FORTRESS
A History of Military Defence

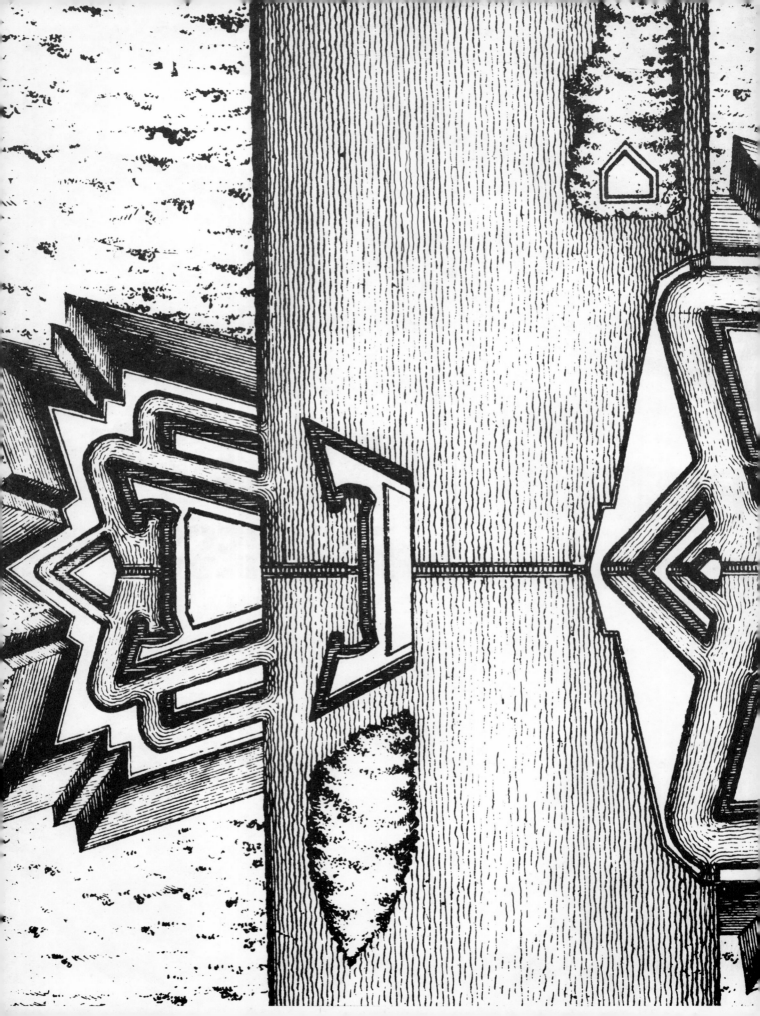

FORTRESS

A History of Military Defence

Ian V. Hogg

St. Martin's Press
New York

For information, write:
St. Martin's Press Inc.,
175 Fifth Ave.,
New York, N.Y. 10010

Printed in the United States of America

First published in the United
    States of America in 1977

Contents

**The origin and Rise of
Fortification is undoubtedly
due to the degeneracy of mankind.**

*J. Muller Professor of Fortification
Royal Military Academy, Woolwich, 1746*

Bibliography

New method of Fortification by Coehorn. *Trans. Savery* 1705

The New Method of Fortification by M. Vauban. *Anon* 1748

Treatise on Fortification *Muller* 1746

Les Science des Ingeneurs. . . *Belidor* 1729

Les Fortifications du Comeedee Pagan *Pagan* 1645

On Fortification *Straith* 1861

Course of Artillery & Fortification *Boxer* 1863

Treatise on Coast Defence *von Sheliha* 1868

Manual de Fortifications de Campagne *Brialmont* n.d.

Paris et ses Fortifications 1870-60 *Tenot* 1881

Mediaeval Military Architecture *Clark* 1884

Our Seacoast Defences *Griffin* 1885

Le Fortification du Temps Present *Brialmont* 1886

Fortification *Clarke* 1890

Armour and its Attack by Artillery *Orde Browne* 1893

Vauban *Blomfield* 1938

The English Castles *D'Auvergne* 1926

The Maginot & Siegfried Lines *Eastwood* 1939

A History of Fortification *Toy* 1955

The Great Wall of France *Rowe* 1959

The Forts of Folly *Eis* 1959

Martello Towers *Sutcliffe* 1972

Coast Defences of England & Wales *Hogg* 1974

Acknowledgements

The assistance of the following individuals and organisations is most gratefully acknowledged; without it the book would have been a good deal less complete.

Michael Jarvis, for his hard work in designing the book, tidying up my sketches until they merit the term 'art work', and for taking many of the photographs.

Peter Chamberlain for photographs of armoured vehicles and German defences.

The Controller of Her Majesty's Stationery Office for permission to reproduce the plan of Chester Castle and the isometric drawing of Dover Castle Keep from 'The History of the King's Works' Vols I and II.

The Illustration Research Service of London for a number of pictures.

Edinburgh University Press for the drawings of Traprain Law Hill Fort and Clickhimin Broch from 'The Iron Age in Northern Britain'.

Cdr. D. P. Kirchner, USN, for information and plans of Japanese and Phillipine coast defences.

Fellow Members of the Fortress Study Group for their various suggestions, comments and items of information.

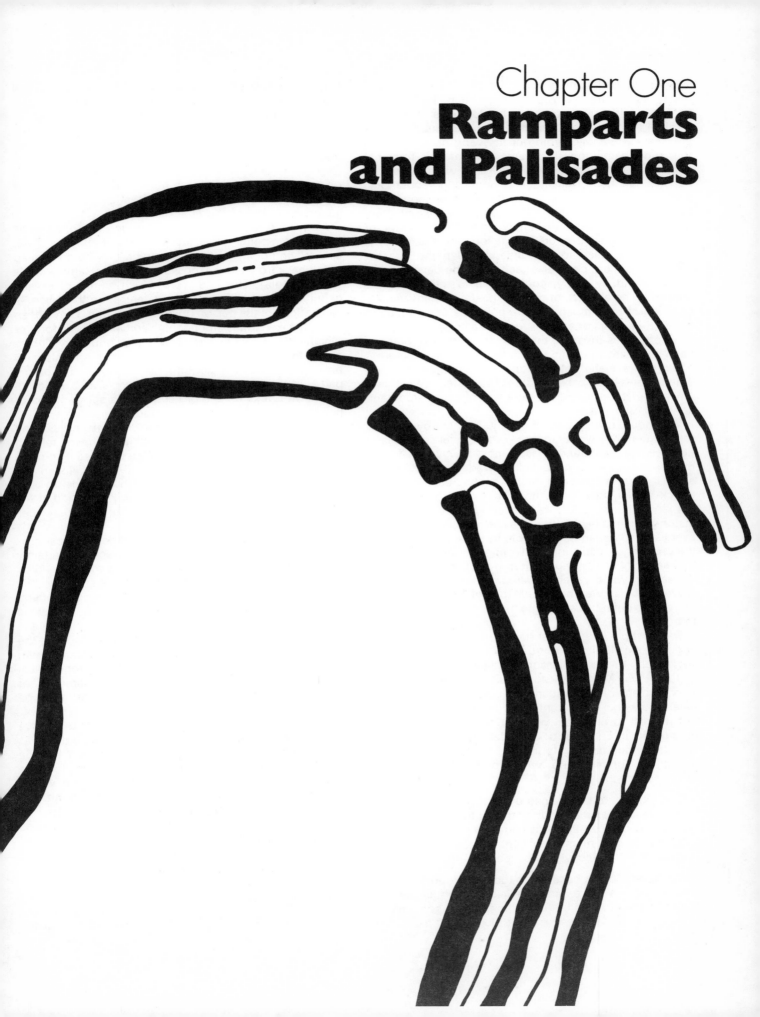

Chapter One
Ramparts and Palisades

The Art of Fortification might be said to have begun when some unknown prehistoric man took shelter behind a fold in the ground, a boulder or a fallen tree-trunk in order to protect himself from the missiles of his adversary while discharging or throwing his own. From this rude beginning it became one of the foremost military arts, gathering complexity as it went, attracting its own language, making and unmaking reputations, and having, if a close analysis is made, apparently insignificant effects upon the course of history. Very rarely has a fortress absolutely denied an invader or attacker his desired course of action; more usually its sole use has been to buy time, to keep the attacker occupied while a counter-attack could be developed or allies, bound by treaty, could come to the aid of the attacked. There exists, of course, the great unanswerable question of how much has the presence of fortification deterred invaders or aggressors from a course of action? How often has the mere threat of some work of defence been sufficient to terminate the thought of war before it could be translated into action? If the number of times when armies have gone headlong into defensive works is any guide, it looks as if the deterrent effect of stone and concrete is minimal.

We should perhaps qualify this judgement by splitting fortification into two branches – coast defence and land defence. Coast defence has, almost always, been the master of its own particular field of warfare, and wherever a coast fortress has been defeated it has been by a land attack which they were never intended to withstand. So far as land warfare is concerned, the teaching of history seems to be that there has never been, nor is there ever likely to be, an impregnable fortress. Fortification is the product of man's ingenuity, and, confronted with it, that same ingenuity, aided often by audacity or reckless endeavour, will invariably overcome the obstacle.

We might as well begin our tour of fortification with one or two definitions, so as to have a firm base on which to build.

Fortification 'is a general name for any work made to oppose a small number of troops against a greater'. Thus spoke John Muller, Professor of Artillery and Fortification at the Royal Military Academy at Woolwich in 1746. This concept of the disparity of forces being aided by defensive works is frequently lost sight of; it is not without interest to note that when, in 1859, a Royal Commission sat in England to 'Consider the Defences of the United Kingdom' they found it salutary to open their report by summing up what fortification might be expected to achieve:

'The Objects to be attained by fortifying any place are (a) to enable a small body of troops to resist a superior force which may attack it; or (b) to enable partially trained bodies of men to contend successfully with those more perfectly disciplined than themselves.'

No exception can be taken to the first proposition; but the second is a snare and a delusion which has caused the downfall of more fortresses than has gunpowder. In the early days of fortress warfare there might have been

some substance to it; everybody on the ramparts [one trained soldier to every five peasants], and when I shout "shoot", fire an arrow at anything you see.' But as defensive works became more complex, the weapons more technical, and the individual more isolated from his fellows; when, by virtue of the ratio of scarce soldiers to length of defensive line more reliance had to be placed on every man, there came a point when the defender's morale and training had to be at least as good as, if not superior to, that of the attacker.

Fortress 'A military position, sited and equipped so as to provide a point of resistance in case of attack, and act as a rallying point for the troops who may be compelled to fall back from more exposed positions' (Harmsworth's Encyclopedia). This is a word which admits of several definitions, depending largely, it seems, on the personal inclinations of the person doing the defining. I have been recently taken to task for defining something as a fortress which did not contain a town within its boundary. Others prefer to apply the name only to a series of defensive positions which are continuously connected. For my part, I incline to a definition of fortress as a series of defensive works for the protection of a specific area or point and under a single command.

As the business of fortification grew, it necessitated the invention of terms for some of its architectural and tactical features, in order to convey a precise meaning in a convenient fashion. These terms will be introduced and explained in their appropriate places; but in order to keep confusion to a minimum, a glossary will be found at the end of the book for those who fall foul of the 'chemin des rondes' en route to the 'fausse braye'.

The development of fortification, while a logical progression, is somewhat confused by the fact that certainly in the early days, the state of the art was conditioned by the degree of civilisation of its practitioners. Thus while the Babylonians and Chaldeans were constructing masonry works of considerable magnitude, at that same time the inhabitants of Britain were still exploring the use of earthwork defences. Therefore, in developing the improvement of defences from the technical standpoint, it becomes necessary to relegate the chronological aspect to a minor place, and a certain amount of oscillation back and forth in time will unfortunately be necessary.

Prehistoric man soon realised that in order to survive the perils of both wild animals and his own kind, it was advisable to locate himself in such a position that he could see the approach of danger and have time to make preparations to counter it, and also a position which placed his assailant at a disadvantage. The summit of a hill answered both purposes; from the summit he had command of the surrounding area and could see enemies approaching far off, and after the enemy scaled the hill he would be fatigued and thus in a disadvantageous condition compared to the rested defender.

From these considerations came the practice of excavating rough earthworks on the tops of convenient hills. In the majority of cases, such sites were inconvenient for the purpose of dwelling and day-to-day

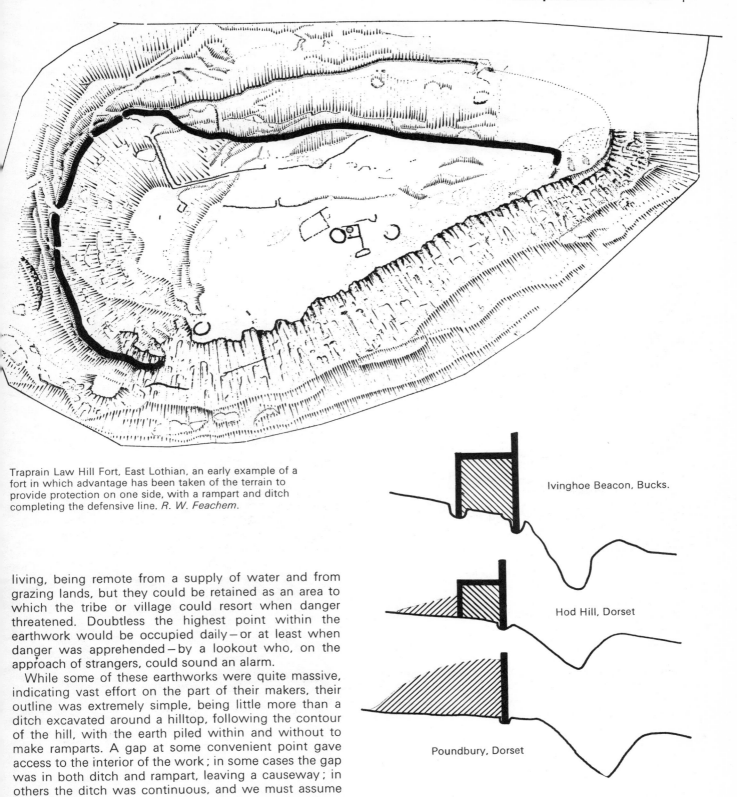

Traprain Law Hill Fort, East Lothian, an early example of a fort in which advantage has been taken of the terrain to provide protection on one side, with a rampart and ditch completing the defensive line. *R. W. Feachem.*

Ivinghoe Beacon, Bucks.

Hod Hill, Dorset

Poundbury, Dorset

Reconstructions of Hill Fort rampart sections.

living, being remote from a supply of water and from grazing lands, but they could be retained as an area to which the tribe or village could resort when danger threatened. Doubtless the highest point within the earthwork would be occupied daily—or at least when danger was apprehended—by a lookout who, on the approach of strangers, could sound an alarm.

While some of these earthworks were quite massive, indicating vast effort on the part of their makers, their outline was extremely simple, being little more than a ditch excavated around a hilltop, following the contour of the hill, with the earth piled within and without to make ramparts. A gap at some convenient point gave access to the interior of the work; in some cases the gap was in both ditch and rampart, leaving a causeway; in others the ditch was continuous, and we must assume the presence of some form of bridge—probably nothing more than a tree-trunk or two—which could be removed when all the occupants were safely inside; or, more simply, that the defenders scrambled across the ditch and up the inner side as best they could. Defence of the

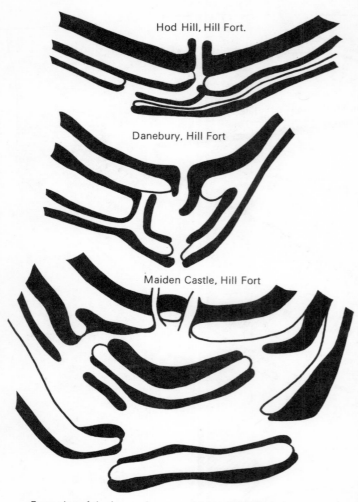

Hod Hill, Hill Fort.

Danebury, Hill Fort

Maiden Castle, Hill Fort

Examples of the increasing complexity of Hill Fort entrances.

Right: Excavation through the ditch of Danebury Hill fort, Hampshire, showing the thickness of the rampart and the difference in level between the interior of the fort and the bottom of the ditch. *David Leigh*.

entrance might have been effected by placing some obstacle – a tree or boulder – in the gap, or, more likely, it was simply a matter of the strongest warriors dealing with the attackers as they were funnelled in by the gap in the rampart. But the basic defence was that the attacker would be at a disadvantage while crossing the ditch and scrambling up the rampart, during which time he was vulnerable to missiles. There was little attempt at subtlety of outline in the excavation in order to put the attacker into some particular position where he would be more than normally vulnerable. Several extant earthworks do, in fact, exhibit various features of construction which suggest such forms of refinement; additional mounds masking the entrance so as to prevent direct approach, or convolutions of the earthwork to channel the attackers into a narrow front, but invariably, archaeological investigation has shown these features to be additions, built several centuries after the original work, when some advance in tactics had been made.

Above: The west entrance complex of Maiden Castle. *Dr. J. K. S. St. Joseph. Crown Copyright reserved.*

Left: An aerial view of Maiden Castle, Dorset. The 160 acres are surrounded by a triple ditch and rampart system. *Dr. J. K. S. St. Joseph. Crown Copyright reserved.*

While such hill earthworks were suitable refuges for large tribes and communities, as the communities spread out and settled the land, they shrank and became too small to put up an effective defence of such large perimeters; Maiden Castle in Dorset, for example, covers some 160 acres, which argues a sizeable defensive force. As a result, smaller works appeared, and eventually a point is reached where a village or a single family demanded a strong-point. It is here that the individual castle begins, originally as an earthwork of similar style, though smaller scale, to the hilltop works, but soon evolving into a form compatible with the location in sites more favourable for day-to-day living if perhaps less tactically suitable.

The original form was simply a mound of earth surrounded by a ditch, the mound being either a natural one selected for the purpose or, more often, constructed by piling up the earth excavated from the ditch. On top of the mound the dwelling was erected, a wooden

A reconstruction of Clickhimin Broch, an early walled homestead of the Picts. The sole entrance was protected by a gatehouse of simple form, and the curtain wall was provided with a banquette for the defenders. *J. R. C. Hamilton.*

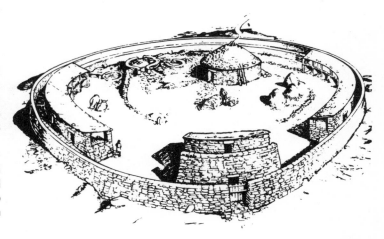

structure, and encircling it was a palisade of wood to form an additional obstacle to any attacker who succeeded in crossing the ditch and scaling the mound.

This type of work is best exemplified in the Norman 'Motte and Bailey' construction; the 'motte' being the mound, and the 'bailey' an outer area surrounding the mound and also enclosed by a second ditch. The bailey was a later addition to the mounded residence and became, in general, the living area for servants and labourers as well as a general refuge for those under the lordship of the owner in times of war. Moreover the bailey formed an additional obstacle, while the motte became the second line of defence; and if the defence of the bailey failed, then the garrison would be withdrawn into the motte to continue resistance or even, after drawing breath, to re-emerge in an attempt to drive out the invaders.

It was this stage of fortification which had been reached in Western Europe, and particularly England, by 1100 AD. But it had long been left behind by other civilisations, and it behoves us now to go back in time, though forward in technology, and consider the use of masonry. And this means a step back of some 3000 years, to consider the defences raised around the great cities of Asia Minor. The Mycenean city of Troy, for example, has revealed remains of masonry city walls with towers and gatehouses built at least 5000 years before Christ. These remains, and others, show that as with the earthwork, the primary demand was for communal protection. A likely reason for the demand is that structures such as city walls were beyond the ability or purse of an individual and required either communal effort or a Royal Exchequer for fulfilment: the walls of Troy were made of stone, and some rose 20 feet in height.

The masonry wall thus marks the first major step in fortification after the earthwork, but a wall is, of itself, a poor defence; therefore these city walls were sufficiently wide to permit the defenders to stand on top so as to be able to launch missiles from the advantage of height. In order to prevent the garrison from inadvertently falling off in the heat of the moment, and to afford them some protection, a parapet was formed behind which the defenders could shelter and over which they could fight. Later, in order to give both better protection and greater facility for discharging arrows, the practice arose of building up sections of wall to a height which would completely protect the defender, and alternating these raised sections with sections of low parapet over which he could shoot, the result, of course, being the familiar 'battlements'.

So long as the attacker kept his distance, the wall was now a reasonable defence, but as the wall became a recognised artifice, so means of defeating it were developed. There were two basic techniques for dealing with a wall defence; either attack the men on top, or attack the fabric of the wall. Attacking the men on top demanded some system of reaching the top from the outside: escalade or climbing the wall by means of ladders was one way, and the use of towers another. The tower would be built alongside the wall, using

Above: Excavations of one of the towers of the Wall of Jericho, illustrating the massive construction. *Jericho Excavation Fund.*
Opposite: The Motte and Bailey work at Pleshey, Essex, an extremely well-preserved example. *Dr. J. K. S. St. Joseph. Crown Copyright reserved.*

archers and spearmen to keep the defenders occupied the while, until it was sufficiently high for a plank bridge to be thrown across to the parapet and allow the attacking party to rush across; it may seem incredible, but with small variations this technique was last used in 1945, as will be told in due course. Or the lower end of the tower might be on wheels or rollers, being built and manned out of bow-shot and then brought up to the wall at some convenient place. Either way meant a fight against odds for the attackers, but even so the technique frequently succeeded.

Dealing with the fabric of the wall might be a longer process but it was likely to be less expensive in men; a party of the attacking force ensconced themselves at the base of the wall and proceeded to pick away at the masonry in the hopes of forming a breach, or the men dug beneath the wall in an attempt to make a tunnel and thus gain entrance to the interior. More ambitious was the technique of mining, or burrowing beneath the foundation of the wall, and shoring it with wooden props until a considerable length had been undermined. Then the mine gallery was packed with combustibles and fired; as the wooden props burned away so the wall above, now devoid of support, crashed down into the

Above: Square towers with reinforced bases in the North-East wall of Dover Castle; beyond them is the Fitzwilliam Gate, and in the ditch is a caponier covering a sally port. *Mike Jarvis.*

Below: A Middle Eastern example of square towers protecting a curtain wall at Montreal Castle, Shubeck, Jordan, dating from the early 12th century. *Jordan Information Service.*

mine, making a breach which the waiting attackers could rush.

These activities against the base of the wall were relatively safe; once hard against the wall, an attacker could only be shot at if a defender leaned well out from the wall — and there would be others of the attacking force positioned to watch for this and deal with it before it could threaten their operators at the wall's foot. It thus became necessary to develop the wall so that its face could be seen and protected. Two systems presented themselves — the hoard and the tower. The hoard was a temporary wooden walk-way built on the outside of the parapet when a siege was threatened. Stones were removed from the parapet to allow beams to be thrust out some 5 or 6 feet, and upon these beams were laid planks, and an outer wall of wood erected in effect, a second parapet was constructed, overhanging the wall. The prime object was to allow the foot of the wall to be covered by the defenders from immediately above: holes in the wooden flooring allowed the downward fire of arrows or the dropping of stones and even the boiling oil so beloved of legend.

The hoard was a suitable protection to be applied to a wall already built, but the tower — built as an integral feature of the wall construction — was the more useful system of protection. By protruding from the face of the wall the tower allowed its occupants to see the wall face

Roman tower and wall at Portchester Castle, incorporated into the later Norman structure. *Mike Jarvis*

and deal with any kind of mining operation; moreover it lent structural strength to the wall. It also divided the wall into sections, so that if the enemy did gain a foothold in one section, he could be confined there and prevented from gaining entry at that spot or moving along the wall to try elsewhere.

The only drawback was that if the tower was square, as the early ones were, it simply meant that the front face of the tower itself became the target, since it could not be seen from the ramparts, and thus the tower had to be hoarded. Another defect of the square tower was the vulnerability of its corners to mining, and the combination of these defects soon led to the adoption of round towers. These, due to their shape, allowed the entire face to be covered by the adjoining walls or adjacent towers. Their resistance to mining was slightly improved due to the absence of vulnerable corners, but in an endeavour to improve matters the base of a round tower was frequently formed into a square by the use of tapering spurs of masonry. This not only produced a wide and firm base but also made the bottom of the tower so immensely thick that the task of effectively mining it became almost impossible.

Above: The Burgess Gate, Denbigh Castle, illustrating the method of reinforcing the tower base by spurs, giving the round tower a more massive base so as to be resistant to mining. *British Tourist Authority*.

Right: The city walls of Avila, Spain, built in 1090–99. *Anne Bolt*.

Walled cities, the curtain wall being reinforced – both structurally and tactically – by towers, became a commonplace before the birth of Christ, and when the basic consideration was the community they survived. Today the majority have crumbled away but one or two of the later examples – proving that the technique of masonry defence took its time to move westward – still exist in France and Spain. The best known is probably Carcassonne in France, but probably the more perfect specimen is Avila in Spain. Avila was built in the last years of the ninth century, the 2-mile circumference of its wall holding no less than eighty-eight towers. Nine defended gates in the wall allow entrance under strict control, and one of the more unusual features is that the city cathedral is so built that its fabric forms part of the wall, the apse forming a tower. Another notable survival is Visby, on the island of Gotland in Sweden, with thirty-eight towers on its walls.

In Europe, however, the rise of the feudal system moved the accent from the walled city to the individual castle, and it was in this field that the development of the more technical aspects of fortification became marked. During the Dark Ages such defensive works as were in existence appear to have been simply remains of Roman or even earlier earthworks, but in the ninth century the depredations of the Normans against the rest of France led to considerable disquiet, and in 862 Charles II, King of the Western Franks (Charles the Bald) authorised the construction of defences at key points in order to resist the Normans. The response of his barons to this was so enthusiastic that within two years he had to issue another edict revoking the first and ordering the

destruction of a large number of castles which had sprung up without benefit of licence. It follows from this that the castles could not have been very large or very ornate, since two years would scarcely have allowed anything very grand to have arisen; the majority of these 'castles' were in fact little more than wooden stockades on a mound, surrounded by a ditch.

With these as a forerunner, the Motte and Bailey castle soon became well established; a mound of anything up to one hundred feet in height, surmounted, as a contemporary noted, by 'a palisade of strong hewn logs strengthened at intervals by as many towers as their means can provide. Inside this enclosure is a citadel or keep. . .'. This was surrounded by the ditch, and beyond

Above: Castle Rising, Norfolk, with the Norman keep in the centre of three earthworks.
Dr. J. K. S. St. Joseph. Crown Copyright reserved.

The rectangular Norman keep of Portchester Castle *Mike Jarvis.*

the ditch was the bailey or outer ward, surrounded in its turn by a ditch and embankment. A bridge gave access to the bailey and another passed from the bailey to the mound. Where the mound was raised artificially — by using the soil excavated from the ditch, supplemented by more from the outer ditch if need be — then, due to its lack of consolidation a wooden structure would be the most that could be expected; but in cases where a natural mound was in a suitable location, it was possible to erect a masonry keep, though the palisade remained of wood.

It was from this basic plan that the masonry castle evolved. The outer ditch surrounding the bailey was replaced by a wall with towers and a wall-walk on top, while the mound and palisade gave way to a stone keep. The size and complexity of the whole work depended very much, of course, on the status of the owner; in the lesser cases the acreage was small and the keep no more than a tower, while in more ornate works covering greater area the keep evolved into the 'shell keep', a circular or polygonal wall with towers, within which the living quarters and stores were built against the wall, leaving an open courtyard in the centre. In many cases the keep was built around the existing mound, the walls passing down the outside to foundations sunk into the virgin earth and the surface of the mound forming an interior floor considerably higher than the surrounding bailey. Even where the floor was at the same level a basic and outstanding tactical feature was the construction of the entrance well above the ground, access being gained by ladders which could be withdrawn or stairs which could be easily defended.

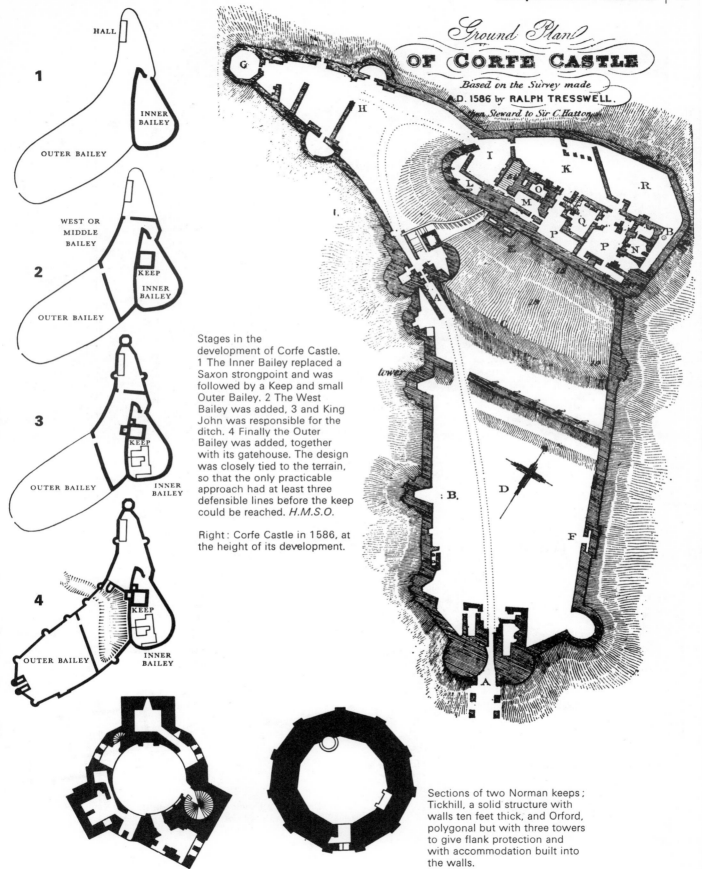

1

HALL

INNER BAILEY

OUTER BAILEY

2

WEST OR MIDDLE BAILEY

KEEP

INNER BAILEY

OUTER BAILEY

3

KEEP

OUTER BAILEY

INNER BAILEY

4

KEEP

OUTER BAILEY

INNER BAILEY

Ground Plan
OF **CORFE CASTLE**
Based on the Survey made
A.D. 1586 by RALPH TRESSWELL.
then Steward to Sir C.Hatton

tower

Stages in the development of Corfe Castle. 1 The Inner Bailey replaced a Saxon strongpoint and was followed by a Keep and small Outer Bailey. 2 The West Bailey was added, 3 and King John was responsible for the ditch. 4 Finally the Outer Bailey was added, together with its gatehouse. The design was closely tied to the terrain, so that the only practicable approach had at least three defensible lines before the keep could be reached. *H.M.S.O.*

Right: Corfe Castle in 1586, at the height of its development.

Sections of two Norman keeps; Tickhill, a solid structure with walls ten feet thick, and Orford, polygonal but with three towers to give flank protection and with accommodation built into the walls.

Above: The Citadel of the Counts of Roussilon at Perpignan. The machicolation is particularly ornate, and there are prominent slots alongside the entrances for the drawbridge balance beams. *French Government Tourist Office.*

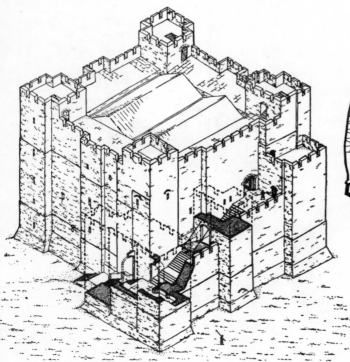

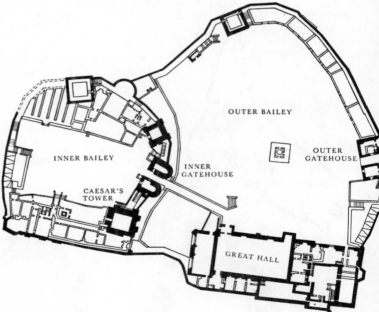

Below left: Dover Castle Keep, illustrating the covered approach to the entrance. *H.M.S.O.*

Below right: Chester Castle in 1769, illustrating the full development of the basic Motte and Bailey configuration. *H.M.S.O.*

Tower of London; a portcullis in the Bloody Tower.
Mike Jarvis.

From this simple formula, subsequent development was largely aimed at rendering assault of the castle ever more difficult. The principle of the hoard was retained in the more permanent form of machicolations, spaced stone buttresses supporting the parapet, the spaces between them permitting the downward discharge it, missiles. The curtain walls grew thicker and higher, and in many cases a second wall was constructed outside it, also with towers, and with its entrance gate some distance away from the gate in the inner work. An assault carrying the outer gate would thus be channelled between the walls where it would be dealt with by archers and spearmen on the parapets.

In order to make the possibility of a break-in even more remote the gate itself ceased to be a simple hole in the wall and became an extremely well-defended unit, covered by towers on its outer side. Instead of opening directly into the interior, the gate now gave access to a courtyard, walled and covered by smaller interior towers, and with an inner gate. The intention was the same, to hold up an assault in a confined space where it could be dealt with at short range. Moreover the actual entrance way became more complicated, with draw-bridges across pits, a portcullis, machicolations over the gateway and flanking arrow-loops covering every inch of the way. The ditch also returned to favour, running all round the curtain wall and was usually filled with water — technically a 'wet ditch' — but inevitably known as a moat, a misnomer arising from the French word 'motte' for the mound within the ditch.

Top right: Dover Castle; a drawbridge at the Palace Gate. In order to provide an obstacle the lifting of the bridge exposed a 'drop' or pit beneath. *Mike Jarvis.*

Below right: Walmer Castle gateway, showing another form of deterrent for attackers, the 'murder holes' through which arrows or firearms could be discharged, or stones or other irritants launched on to the heads of the intruders. *Mike Jarvis.*

Opposite page.

Below left: Portchester Castle; portion of the inner ward, showing the entrance gateway and inner ditch. *Mike Jarvis.*

Top: Portchester Castle; the entrance to the inner ward seen from the outer bailey, the inner ditch in the foreground. *Mike Jarvis.*

Below right: Tower of London; part of the curtain wall, showing arrow loops and crenellation. *Mike Jarvis.*

Page 24: Fiennes's Tower or Constable's Gate, Dover Castle. A powerful complex of five towers, it was built after the siege of 1216 and considerably added to in the 18th century. *Mike Jarvis.*

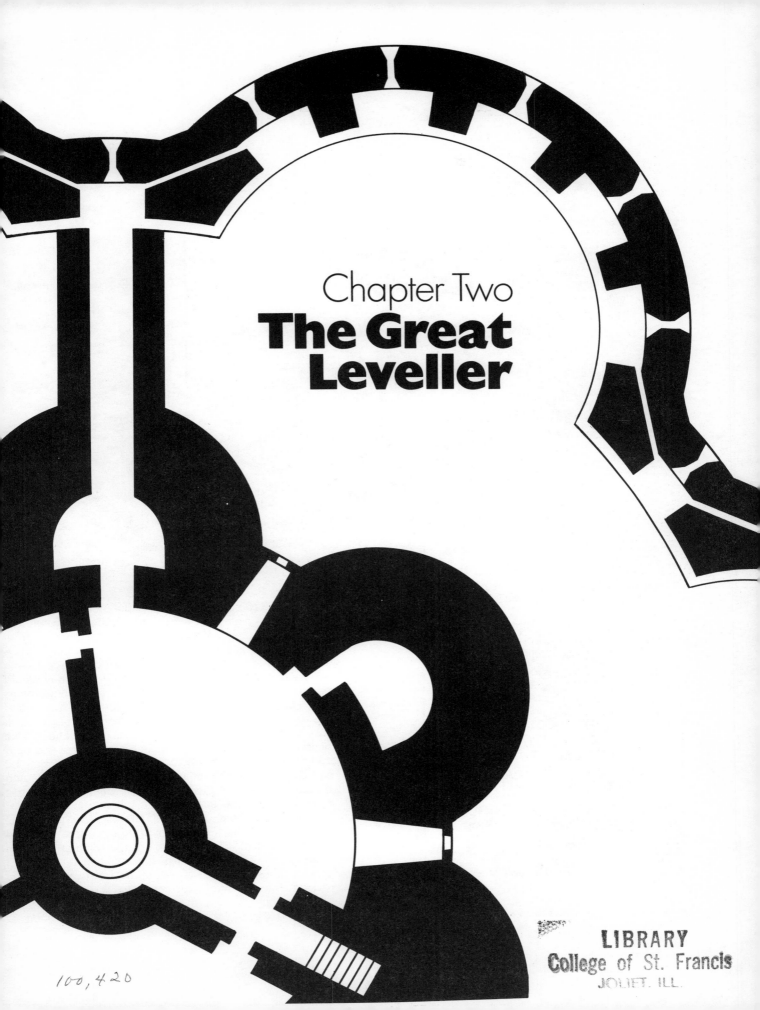

Chapter Two
The Great Leveller

An example of a pre-artillery siege, the besiegers using a tower and the defenders attempting to put it out of action with a catapult

Another example of a beffroy or tower in use; this serves two purposes, to place the attackers on top of the wall and also to cover the use of a ram to break in the wall.

In about 1325 some unknown experimenter discovered that by using a black powder compounded from sulphur, saltpetre and charcoal, he could discharge a missile from a tube closed at one end. The cannon was born.

What evidence there is of early cannon suggests that the weapons were employed solely in what today would be called the anti-personnel role, but the effect was as much moral as physical. For the first forty or fifty years of the cannon's life the fact that the device worked at all was sufficient cause for wonder; its noise and smoke overawed the superstitious, scared the horses, and now and then the discharged missile actually killed or maimed someone. But as the weapon became more reliable and the gunners more skilled, the firearm began its slow rise to supremacy. The early cannon were small, of one or two inches calibre, and fired arrows with the shafts bound with leather thus steadying them in the bore and also giving a rudimentary seal for the powder gases to push against. Then lead or iron balls became the standard projectile, and the gun-arrow fell into disuse, not to be revived until the twentieth century.

Within thirty years of the introduction of artillery to the battlefield there is a record of the first association of

Above: A siege in the late 15th century, one of the earliest depictions of cannon against fortification. The work at the left appears to be a temporary structure; behind it is a cannon on a wooden bed. *Trustees of the British Museum.*

cannon and castle; in 1356 an English garrison in Breteuil was besieged by the French Army of King John. The French filled in the ditch, crossed it, and brought up a 'beffroy' or fighting tower to the wall. The defenders first engaged the assaulting party by the traditional methods of hand-to-hand fighting, but then withdrew suddenly, allowing gunners to open fire on the 'beffroy' with cannon, discharging both arrows and 'jets of fire', which disposed of the assaulting troops and set fire to the tower into the bargain. There is some doubt as to whether the chronicler was referring to the muzzle flash from the guns or whether they were, in some fashion, being used to discharge the celebrated 'Greek Fire' type of composition; although quite definite in the matter of the 'jets of fire', the chronicler gives no explanation as to how it was done.

The first mention of the use of cannon in an attack on a castle seems to be found in the *Cronica di Pisa*, written at the end of the fourteenth century. This records that in 1362, when the Pisans were besieging the castle of Pietra Buona, they employed a 'bombard' weighing 2000 lbs, but there is no record of its effect on the castle. Three years later though, in 1365, the citizens of Chartres, who had purchased some cannon in 1357, lent them to the Duke of Burgundy; by using these, and a number of siege engines, the Duke captured the Castle of Camrolles and presented it to Chartres by way of a hiring fee for the weapons. This more than satisfied the citizens, since the occupants of the castle had been a thorn in their side for some years.

A few more years and 1369 sees a record of cannon being used to protect the town gates of Arras; the register of accounts notes the provision of one cannon, twelve arrows and a supply of powder to each of various gates. It would seem likely that these weapons would be mounted above or alongside the gate, where movement in and out could be observed, and used entirely as an anti-personnel weapon. Then in 1374 the King of France's Lieutenant in Lower Normandy engaged a 'cannoneer' for fifteen gold pieces a month 'to make certain large cannon throwing stones and fire them as often as might be required at the Siege of St Sauveur le Vicomte', but again, there is no record of what effect his cannon might have had.

Very soon, however, cannon began to increase in size, and in 1377 at the Siege of Odruik, Froissart records that

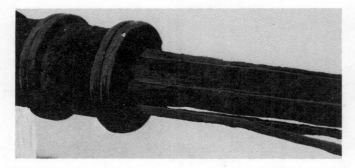

An example of early cannon construction, showing the longitudinal strips and circumferential hoops. *Mike Jarvis*.

140 cannon were used by the Duke of Burgundy, some of which fired projectiles of 200 lbs in weight, equating to a bore of 16.5 inches or so. The important thing about this siege is that the records speak of the walls of the castle being pierced by these stone projectiles, a circumstance which led to its surrender by William de Weston, the English commander. This is the first recorded case of artillery being employed against the fabric of a work rather than against the defenders, the first record of artillery achieving a breach in the walls, and the first record of artillery bringing about the surrender of a castle. Projectiles of this, and greater, weight had, of course, been discharged by engines in previous times, but the flatter trajectory and greater striking velocity attained by cannon shot, even with the poor gunpowder and weak guns of the day, made for greater kinetic effect at the target. The lesson was certainly not lost on the Duke of Burgundy, for immediately after the siege he set his 'cannoneers' to work to produce a gun capable of firing a 450-lb stone shot, equivalent to a calibre of about 21 inches. The particular application or purpose for which this weapon was intended appears to have escaped record, but from that time onward there are numerous references to cannon of extremely large calibre firing heavy weights of shot, and these could only have been intended for the attack of castles.

One of the best examples of the employment of the early cannon in siege warfare is in the War of Chiogga, between the Venetians and the Genoese in 1379–80. There was a considerable use of 'bombards' by both sides, and in January 1380 the Venetians set up a battery of these guns, firing stone balls weighing from 140 to 200 lbs each, to attack Brondolo. One 200-lb stone shot struck the campanile of Brondolo and brought down a stretch of wall, killing twenty-two men in the collapse. Admittedly this was a monastery and not a castle, but the material and construction appear to have been roughly comparable with many castles of the day, and after a few more days of bombardment the monastery was completely ruined.

This sort of performance was becoming commonplace at the start of the fifteenth century, and it is all the more remarkable when one considers the state of the gunner's art at that time. The gunpowder of the day was a weak composition, finely ground so that it tended to consolidate in the gun and resist efficient ignition, which led to slow combustion, low velocities and unpredictable trajectories. The guns themselves were of weak construction, usually of longitudinal iron strips surrounded by hoops, bound by rope, and frequently finished off with rawhide stitched around them to preserve the iron and rope from damp. These guns were fitting companions to their powder had the powder been more efficient the guns would have burst asunder and the development of artillery might have been abandoned as being altogether too hazardous an enterprise.

Nevertheless, the cannon was capable of breaching the contemporary castle; of that there is no doubt. Previous to the cannon the only breaching methods had been the battering ram and the mine: both could be foiled to some degree by making the wall thick at the base; but above the height at which a ram could operate, the wall was often much thinner in section, and as high as was thought necessary to discourage attempts at escalade, the use of towers, and high enough to repel the missiles hurled by all but the largest throwing engines. But the cannon now made nonsense of these defences; the wall needing to be resistant to shot for its full height. No longer was the base the only area at risk. The gunner could breach at any point he chose, and then by successive shots enlarge the breach downward to a point where foot soldiers could escalade and enter. The greater the height, the better the target indeed, as more masonry was liable to collapse after a breach was made. And no longer did height serve to confound engines, since the engine gradually fell into disuse.

As a result of these considerations, the latter part of the fifteenth century saw the birth of castles designed with a view to resisting attack by artillery. The first of this class, certainly in Britain if not in Europe, was Ravenscraig,

Southsea Castle embrasure battery. *Mike Jarvis*

By the 15th century the wheeled carriage was beginning to appear among the besieger's armament. *Trustees of the British Museum*.

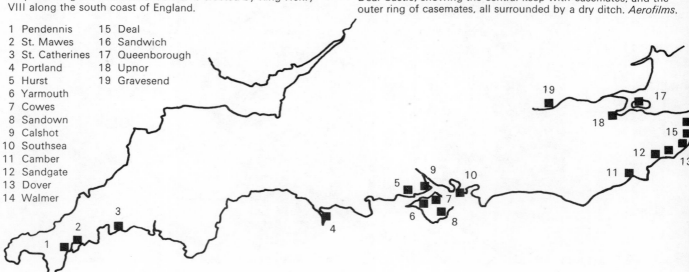

Map showing the coast defence works erected by King Henry VIII along the south coast of England.

Deal Castle, showing the central keep with casemates, and the outer ring of casemates, all surrounded by a dry ditch. *Aerofilms*.

1 Pendennis
2 St. Mawes
3 St. Catherines
4 Portland
5 Hurst
6 Yarmouth
7 Cowes
8 Sandown
9 Calshot
10 Southsea
11 Camber
12 Sandgate
13 Dover
14 Walmer
15 Deal
16 Sandwich
17 Queenborough
18 Upnor
19 Gravesend

near Dysart in Fife, built in 1460, but thereafter many more sprang up, the last of the type, it is generally conceded, being that of Malmö in Sweden, completed in 1542. The general characteristic of these castles is their immensely thick walling – Salses in France has walls 70 feet thick – and their rather squat appearance. Another feature often found is a tower of large diameter upon which defensive artillery could be mounted behind a parapet and fire through embrasures – what might be called the artillery equivalent of battlements.

Making a castle structure resistant to artillery was only half the battle – the other half was integrating artillery into the defensive arrangements, and while the artillery towers mentioned above made a gesture in this direction, they were little more than the adaptation of existing technique to try and take advantage of the gun. The first integrated designs of works which took the various functions of artillery into full account were undoubtedly the coast defence castles built in England by Henry VIII beginning in 1539. These were built to cover the Channel coast from Kent to Cornwall, plus one (Castle Cornet) in Guernsey; in addition, one or two existing castles, such as those at Dover and Dartmouth, were adapted so as to copy the basic features.

The new castles broke completely fresh ground; they were solid, compact blocks capable of all-round defence and dispensed with the combination of walls and towers. The basis was generally a cylindrical central tower surrounded by half-round bays resembling shortened towers. Within these, guns were mounted in casemates, vaulted chambers with gun ports allowing the gun muzzle to protrude and the gun to be swung from side to side within the casemate to cover a wide arc with fire. More guns were mounted on the casemate roofs,

A Flemish bronze gun of 1607, typical of the armament of fortified places at that time. *Mike Jarvis.*

Varieties of cannon, as depicted in a 17th century text.

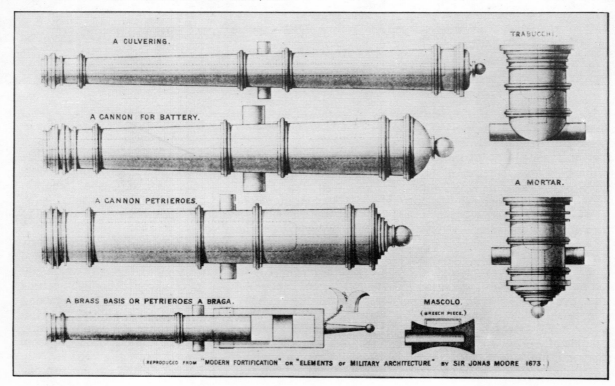

A CULVERING.

TRABUCCHI.

A CANNON FOR BATTERY.

A CANNON PETRIEROES.

A MORTAR.

A BRASS BASIS OR PETRIEROES A BRAGA.

MASCOLO.
(BREECH PIECE.)

(REPRODUCED FROM "MODERN FORTIFICATION" OR "ELEMENTS OF MILITARY ARCHITECTURE" BY SIR JONAS MOORE 1673.)

while the central tower, or keep, was self-defensible, with guns on the roof and in casemates so that they could not only aid in defending the work but could also if necessary sweep the tops of the outer casemate structures.

The precise construction varied from castle to castle. Deal is probably the most symmetrical, having a central tower surrounded by six casemates at middle level, surrounded in turn by a further six larger casemates at a lower level. The whole is surrounded by a ditch conforming to the outline of the lower level of casemates. The whole work is a cohesive mass. St Mawes, on the other hand, has a central tower surrounded by four immensely thick curved wall units, with the casemates formed within these walls, the rear of the casemates backing on to an open space around the keep. Walmer Castle has been considerably modified over the years, as a consequence of its being adopted as the official residence of the Lord Warden of the Cinque Ports; but Deal, after undergoing renovation and the removal of various odd structures which have appeared on its roof over the years, is now substantially as Henry intended it, and amply repays examination. The internal arrangements were as well thought out as the external, and any would-be assailant would have had a difficult time even had he gained entrance via the single door: drawbridge, portcullis, a trapdoor covering a pit in the entrance, angled passages covered by firing ports for hand guns — every artifice that could be employed was used to good effect.

Walmer Castle; one of the casemates, showing the musketry ports on the lower level and the port for a defensive cannon above. *Mike Jarvis*

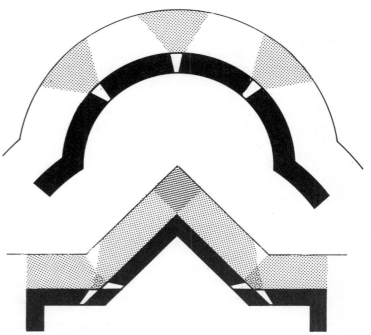

A comparison of the bastions of Deal Castle (top) and Southsea Castle (below) illustrating the improvement in fields of fire, the Southsea bastion giving complete protection to all faces of the work

The thing which singles out Henry's castles from most other coastal works — of that or any other day — is their self-sufficiency. The theory of their operation was based on the superiority of shore armament over contemporary ship armament. The heaviest piece commonly found on a ship in the sixteenth century was the 18-pounder culverin, while the forts were provided on their sea faces with the 32-pounder demi-cannon. The theoretical maximum range of the demi-cannon might have been fractionally less than that of the culverin, but their effective range, the range at which accurate and damaging fire could be brought to bear, was superior and, moreover, since the guns were securely mounted in a stone casemate their service was easier and their fire much more accurate than was the case for the gun out at sea. As a result, the coast fort was the master of the ships within its purview : the only way a ship could approach the land would have been to do so with the assistance of a land force. Such a force, landed elsewhere out of the reach or sight of the fort and marching overland to take the fort in rear and neutralise it would have been a possible tactical manoeuvre. But Henry's forts were designed with this manoeuvre in mind : their all-round fire capability using 18-pounder culverins and 9-pounder demi-culverins, their ditch and their whole arrangement effectively ruling out any chance of a successful land-side attack except by an organised army with accompanying cannon.

Henry deserves very great credit for appreciating something which many fortress designers overlooked in subsequent years ; that the only way to reduce a coastal work is to attack it from the land side. History is replete with examples of this manoeuvre, and the twentiety century particularly rich in them, from Port Arthur to Cherbourg by way of Singapore, Oslo and Bataan.

Deal Castle ; the keep, seen from the inner ditch. It can be seen that the ditch was thoroughly covered by musketry or short range cannon fire from the casemates, and that capture of the outer ring of casemates was by no means the end of the affair. *Mike Jarvis*.

Top : Southsea Castle ; Henry's original keep and outer battery, an unusually angular design. The darker section of parapet at the left is a Victorian modification for a barbette battery. *Mike Jarvis*.

Chapter Three
The Entry
of the Masters

The arrival of artillery took some time to make its effect completely felt; the absolute effect, the smashing power of the shot, the random execution dealt out on all sides, was fairly rapidly appreciated and had its results in the gradual decline of the armoured and mounted knight. An effect which took much longer to develop was the appreciation that there were other ways of achieving results with cannon than by simply positioning them in front of a work and battering until something gave way. This delay in the advance of gunnery was principally due to the limitations imposed by the ordnance. They were heavy and cumbersome, difficult, if not impossible, to move with the speed needed to keep up with the flow of battle, and in siege actions they were simply put down at a convenient point as close to the selected point of breach and that was all. Only in siege warfare, indeed, could the gunner look forward to firing more than one or two shots, since in the normal run of battles the charge of cavalry or surge of infantry usually rolled past the guns after the first volley and left them with little to do. At least in a siege there was the likelihood of spending a week or two in the same place.

During the fifteenth century three steps were taken which helped to improve the cannon and with this the effectiveness of artillery. Firstly, the gunpowder was improved by developing a technique known as 'corning' in which the ingredients were mixed wet, dried into a cake and then crumbled and passed through sieves to produce a granular powder of even size. This meant that the charge, when loaded into the gun, was less densely

An engraving of a siege, c. 1485, by Israhel van Meckenen. The breech-loading guns have been left while the besiegers repel a sortie from the besieged place.

Right: A 17th century mortar on its bed. *Mike Jarvis.*

Opposite: Mahomet's Great Gun, typical of Turkish ordnance of the Middle Ages, and cast for use in the Siege of Constantinople. Cast in two sections, breech and barrel, which screw together. *Mike Jarvis.*

packed and allowed the ignition flame to pass quickly through the mass. This gave more rapid combustion and faster generation of gas, leading to a more powerful result. Unfortunately it was also more violent and frequently blew the early cannon to pieces, for which reason it was, at first, little used. In the latter part of the century the second material improvement was initiated by mastering the technique of casting iron cannon. This permitted stronger weapons which could withstand the firing of corned powder, and from then on the power of guns began to make a steady advance.

The third significant feature of the 1400's was the development of the mortar, a cannon which fired its projectiles up into the air in a high trajectory so as to drop them behind walls or other defences, which the flat trajectory of the cannon could not reach. The first use of the mortar was connected with siege work in a roundabout way; a manuscript by a Greek, Kritoboulos, written in 1467, describes Mohammed II's siege of Constantinople in 1453.

An early engraving of a mortar
in use against a castle.

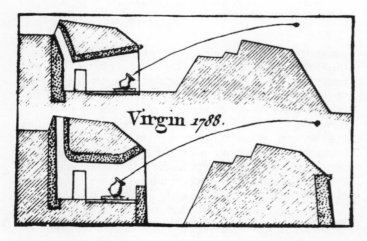

Virgin 1788.

Defensive mortars emplaced within a form of casemate so as to
give the best possible cover while still allowing them to fire.

A fleet of Turkish vessels attempting to enter the
Golden Horn were repulsed by a chain barrier and guard
vessels, whereupon 'The Emperor beholding the repulse
of this attack turned his attention to the invention of
another machine. He called together all those who made
his guns and demanded of them if it were not possible to
fire upon the ships anchored at the entrance to the port
so as to sink them to the bottom. They made answer
that there were no cannon capable of producing such an
effect, adding that the walls of Galata hindered them on
all sides.

'The Emperor then proposed to them a different mode
of proceeding and a totally new description of gun, of
which the form should be a little modified so as to enable
it to throw its shot to a great height that in falling it might
strike the vessel in the middle and sink her. He explained
to them in what manner, by certain proportions calculated and based on analogy, such a machine would act
against shipping. And these on reflection saw the
possibility of the thing, and they made a species of
cannon after the outline the Emperor had made for them.

'Having next considered the ground, they placed it a

little below the Galata Point on a ridge which rose a little opposite the ships. Having placed it well and pointed it in the air according to the proper calculations, they applied the match and the mortar threw its stone to a great height, then falling, it missed the ships the first time and pitched very near them into the sea. Then they changed the direction of the mortar a little and threw a second stone. This, after rising to an immense height, fell with a great noise and violence and struck a vessel amidships, shattered it, sunk it to the bottom, killed some of the sailors and drowned the rest, only a few saved themselves by swimming to the other ships and nearer galleys.'

While the mortar was not destined to play much part in siege warfare for some years, the improvements in cannon leading to lighter and more powerful weapons, together with the adoption of the wheeled carriage, allowed the artillery to be moved rather more readily, and some fresh techniques appeared. One of the fundamental discoveries was the advantage to be gained by siting a gun in prolongation of a defensive line, so that it could be fired along the line; if it missed the nearer defenders, the further it went the more chance it had of striking others beyond, and a single ball would do a vastly disproportionate amount of damage. This was 'enfilade' or 'flanking' fire, and in those days of slow-loading guns it gave a useful accretion to fire-power. As much as anything else it was the problem of enfilade which led to the next series of advances in fortification; the question being one of how to protect against being enfiladed while adopting positions calculated to give the best chance of enfilading an enemy. And this marks the virtual obsession with flanking which almost obscures every other defensive consideration for the next three centuries.

The improvement in fortification also signalled a move away from the private castle to the state fortress. This again, while doubtless accelerated by social development, was also due to the power of artillery. Few feudal lords could afford the cost of an immensely thick castle to defend himself against cannon, and, equally so, few could afford artillery for its defence. Due to the expense of cannon and the retinue of specialists to operate and support them, plus the cost of supplying ammunition, warfare became the prerogative of kings and states rather than a matter of petty quarrels among rival barons. As a result, the military engineer found an outlet for his talents in the construction of works of defence for the state, the only body who could afford such structures and arm them once built.

The fundamental structural feature which distinguishes an artillery-oriented fort from a work of pre-artillery days is the 'bastion', an angular projection which largely replaced the tower as a system of wall protection. The precise definition of a bastion is 'A work composed of two faces and two flanks . . . constructed so that the whole escarp may be seen.' The escarp, for the moment, can be taken to be the face of the curtain wall in between the bastions, so that it becomes plain that the bastion took over the tower's function of covering the faces of

the work. But since the sides of the bastion were straight, and since it projected some distance, it was possible to mount a number of guns on the bastion to cover the wall face with heavy fire rather than attempt to cover it with one or two guns, which would be all the tower would have managed. Moreover the bastion allowed flanking fire to be delivered to the face, but, by its orientation, prevented flanking fire from an enemy from doing much damage: if an enemy positioned a gun so as to flank the face of the work, it would not flank the faces of the bastion, and, due to the bastion, its effect would be severely localised. Were the enemy to flank the line of the bastion, his fire would not flank anything else, and again the effect would be limited.

Exactly who invented the bastion is open to some doubt, but it is generally accepted that the idea originated in Italy; one of the oldest known bastioned works is that of the outer defences of Verona, built by an Italian engineer Michele San Michele in 1523, though Papacino d'Antoni, Professor of Fortification at Turin, stated in his *Architectur Militari* of 1759 that small bastions had been constructed in the fifteenth century, and a recent work refers to a bastioned fort at Nettuno, ascribed to Sangallo and tentatively dated at 1501. Another Italian, Paciotto d'Urbino, built the citadel of Antwerp for Charles V in 1545 and employed the bastion in his construction; they were small and widely spaced, but nevertheless exhibited the basic features.

By the latter end of the sixteenth century the Italians were the most prominent fortress engineers in the world, and they had, by the beginning of the seventeenth century, given shape to every major architectural feature of land fortification which was to be subsequently used. In 1564 Jacomo Castriotto published a book on fortification in which the use of bastions, cavaliers, ramparts, covered ways, orillons and glacis were laid down and illustrated, and the powerful fortress of Lucca, close to Pisa, exhibits almost every contemporary feature of the period since it was under construction from about 1535 (authorities differ on this point) to 1649.

It has been averred that the basis of the Italian system was not the cannon, but the musket, and there is a certain amount of justification for this view. The early fortress builders were principally concerned with the effect of heavy ordnance, but the first half of the sixteenth century saw the introduction of the wheel-lock and the second half the introduction of the flint-lock, both of which were major steps in improving the reliability, rapidity and accuracy of shoulder arms. As a result the musket became a prime defensive weapon: it became necessary to produce space for musketeers and, as will be seen later, the basic dimensions of a work were frequently dictated less by the terrain as by the fighting range of the contemporary musket, so that the bastions of a work lay within easy musket shot of each other.

The practice of constructing massive masonry walls as a defence against battering by artillery was recognised by the logical Italians as being wasteful of time, money and materials: furthermore, masonry was not the best material with which to resist such a battering, since the

Top: An early matchlock; more common than the wheelock, since it was less mechanically involved. Pressure on the trigger pulled the burning slowmatch back to ignite the powder in the vent. *Ian Hogg.*

Centre: The flintlock; more rapid in action, more certain than the matchlock, it revolutionised firearms. *Ian Hogg.*

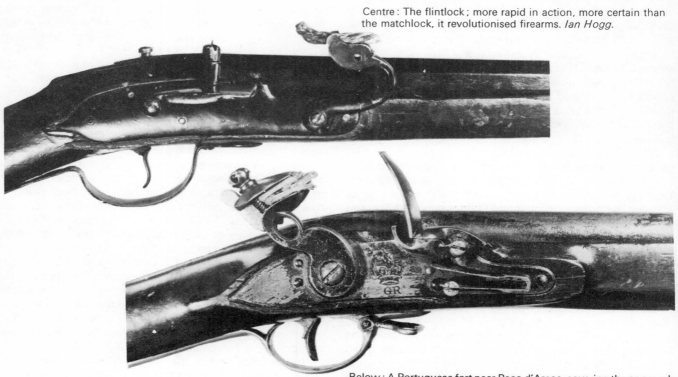

Below: A Portuguese fort near Paco d'Arcos, covering the approach to Lisbon *Ian Hogg*

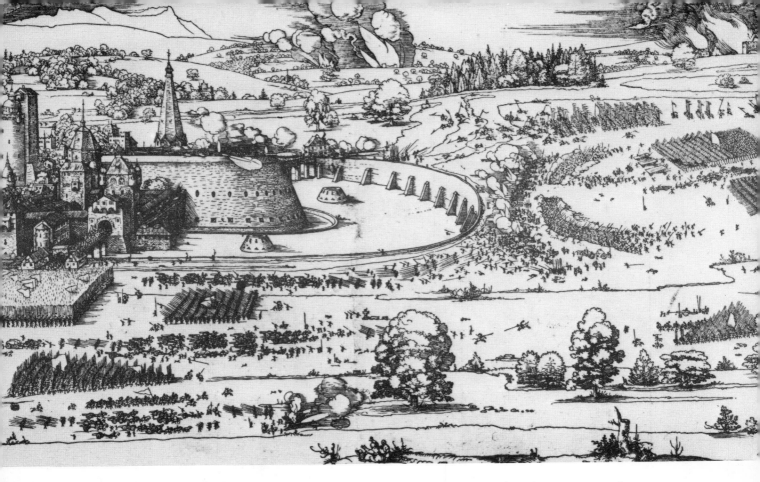

strike of the shot broke and splintered the face of the stone. Far better, they decided, to provide banks of earth which were cheaper, demanded no skilled masons or other expensive specialists for their construction, and absorbed artillery fire like a sponge absorbing water. From this reasoning the rampart of earth re-appeared, and with it the ditch, the latter providing the material for the former, a process later known as 'deblai and remblai'; deblai was the term given to the mass of earth in the ditch before being excavated, and remblai being the same mass of earth after it had been built up into the work. With the rampart thus thrown up, it became necessary to so profile the summit as to provide the musketeers with a suitable firing position while allowing them some protection, and the rampart was surmounted by a parapet behind which men could take cover and over which they could shoot.

A certain amount of masonry was still required, however, to face the side of the ditch beneath the rampart; were the ditch to be cut at the natural slope of fall of the earth, its effectiveness as an obstacle would be lessened, so by cutting it vertically and supporting it with a wall the defensive aspect was improved. By the same token, the rampart face needed to be vertical to offer the greatest obstacle, to secure the earth of the rampart and to utilise the ground to the best advantage: obviously a rampart with the front and rear faces at the natural angle of fall of the earth would occupy almost twice the ground area of one with the outer face vertical, or at least steeply sloped and with a retaining wall. There is also the point that many of the Italian engineers

learned their trade and improved their skills while making improvements to earlier works by erecting earthen ramparts behind the existing stone walls, a practice which may very well have led them directly to a wall-retained structure without necessarily ever contemplating wholly earth ramparts.

It would be as well, at this point, to bring forward two names whose influence on fortification and military engineering is a matter of unresolved discussion: Leonardo da Vinci and Albrecht Dürer. Da Vinci, a man of many parts to say the least, produced a number of drawings of fortifications, but none of them stand up to critical analysis. His interest in the subject was ephemeral, and he appears to have approached the matter rather more as a theoretical exercise in architectural design than with any appreciation of tactics or fire-power. His 'Drawing of a Bastion' in the *Codex Atlanticus*, for example, is a half-section of a circular fort with two ditches and with blockhouses on the rampart, accompanied by a sketch of a form of casemate and a rather peculiar tower to be placed in the ditch and connected by subterranean tunnels to the interior of the fort. There appears to be no means of mounting guns on the ramparts — though doubtless he would have readily designed a machine for the purpose had he been asked — and the work is entirely devoid of flank protection.

Dürer, an architect amongst his other abilities, produced a number of more interesting designs. His approach

Above: Carisbrooke Castle, Isle of Wight; Gianibelli's artillery bastions are in the foreground. *Aerofilms.*
Right: Naarden, Holland, a particularly fine example of the Dutch Bastioned System and its use of water. Most of the causeways entering the town are modern additions. *K.L.M. Ltd.*

began with the round tower, which he considerably enlarged and called 'Bastei' – in the plural 'Basteien', and doubtless with some bearing on the word 'bastion – and his basic principle was that the cannon mounted on these basteien were only of use when the enemy was at a distance. Once they closed on the work, defence was taken over by casemates or vaulted galleries within the body of the rampart, with additional vaulted works, which later became known as 'caponiers,' passing across the ditch so as to deliver fire down the length of the ditch against any attackers who entered it. Unfortunately the designs ran to extremes of giantism; the basteien were over 130 yards in diameter, with their faces 120 feet high, fronting a ditch 100 feet wide, and these impractical dimensions led to his ideas being ignored by practical engineers, who wrote him off as a visionary. Although no work was ever built according to Dürer's ideas, if his designs are scaled down to manageable proportions they will be seen to contain numerous practical ideas, and certainly his espousal of casemates and caponiers was several hundred years ahead of its time.

Another interesting speculation which has been advanced is that Italian engineers were responsible for the design and construction of Henry VIII's coast defence castles discussed in the previous chapter. I take leave to doubt this; had such an engineer been imported, he would undoubtedly have taken the opportunity to exhibit his proficiency in the latest state of the art, and since the angular bastion was by that time an existing fact and moderately well-known among the Italians, it seems unlikely that such an engineer would have built in the

circular form. Certainly one Italian was imported at the end of the century to bring an important work up to the highest contemporary standard of defence. In 1588 the threat of the Spanish Armada led to a hurried refurbishing of defences along the English coast, and one of the areas in which it was expected that the Spanish would land was the Isle of Wight. Although the immediate danger passed with the destruction of the Armada, the following years saw a great deal of improvement of defences, and in 1598 or thereabouts one Federigo Gianibelli was brought to England in order to improve the defences of Carisbrooke Castle.

Carisbrooke began its career as a Roman fort and was then overlaid by a Norman motte and bailey work. In the twelfth century it was improved by surrounding the bailey with a wall and erecting a shell keep on the motte. It was subsequently improved and added to by its various owners. Gianibelli left the basic structure more or less untouched, but enlarged the ditch and built two large bastions on the south side, facing the expected line of approach of invasion, and provided these bastions with ramparts behind which artillery could be mounted. So far as can be ascertained this was all the work the visitor was asked to do, and Carisbrooke remains the only bastioned work of its kind in England.

With the dismemberment of Italy in the late sixteenth century, when it became, to quote Metternich, 'a mere geographical expression' instead of a nation, most of the Italian engineers departed to other countries to find employment for their talent, and their mastery began to wane. Most of them appear to have gone to France where they were instrumental in training the next generation of fortress engineers who initiated the rise of French influence in this field. Others went to Spain and Holland, thus finding themselves on opposing sides, and those in the employ of the Dutch were largely responsible for laying the foundations of the fortification system which became peculiar to that country, relying as it did upon water defences.

The Italian engineer Marchi, who went to Holland in 1559, appears to have been the innovator of this system which, since the water table of the Netherlands was but a few feet below the surface, precluded much use of ditches or other subterranean work. As a result, the Dutch Bastioned System was exemplified, as at Breda, by wide wet ditches surrounding unrevetted earthen ramparts. These were relatively low — mere parapets in fact — though of considerable thickness, and behind them were open spaces. Behind each space rose the main rampart of the work. The small parapet alongside the ditch — called the 'fausse braye' — was the first line of defence, and the open space behind it — the 'chemin des rondes' (from which came the anglicised expression 'making the rounds' or inspecting the defences in the chemin des rondes) — served as a covered place for the assembly and movement of troops during a siege. Should the attack cross the ditch and overcome the first line, the defenders could retreat through various gates into the main work to continue resistance from the main ramparts.

One of the first French engineers to come to prominence, if we exclude one or two eccentrics who broke into print, was Jean Errard of Bois-le-Duc. He was one of the principal officers of the King's Engineers-in-Ordinary, a corps formed by the Duc de Sully who was Grand Master of Artillery under Henry IV. In 1597, on Sully's command, Errard published a book on Fortification which became the standard text of the time, running into four editions. Errard was a soldier, a man who had seen considerable active service and brought a sound appreciation of tactics and contemporary weapon capability to the problems of defence; he was responsible for works at Doullens, Amiens, Montreuil and Calais.

Errard's principle was to defend inwards; in other words, having established the 'trace' of the work — its outline on the ground — he used this to delineate the line of the ditch and then, moving inwards, established the line of the rampart and added his bastions. At that time there was considerable argument about how the flanks of a bastion should be designed; at right-angles to the rampart where they joined it, or at right-angles to the faces of the bastion, meeting the rampart at an acute angle. Errard was not dogmatic about this; in works of eight or less faces he made the flank perpendicular to the face of the bastion, but where a work had nine or more faces, then he made it perpendicular to the rampart. He was alive to the possibilities of flanking fire, but he appears to have concentrated his defence on the ramparts and left his ditch to look after itself.

Errard was succeeded by the Chevalier Antoine de Ville, another widely travelled and practical soldier. He was responsible for a large 'Traité des Fortifications', and claimed that there was nothing therein except that which either he or his brother had seen or done. Unfortunately one must discount this claim, since it was published when he was but 33 years of age and, from other remarks and observations in the text, it appears that he began assembling the work when he was only 21. Nevertheless it was an exceptionally useful text and it became the standard work of the times. His system of fortification became known as the 'French Method' or 'Compound System' since it united the earlier Spanish and Italian methods and overlaid them with some native observations and much of Errard's work.

De Ville appears to have been the first to bring geometry and proportion into his designs, a fashion which, in due course, appears to take precedence over tactical considerations and was largely responsible for numerous scornful observations on the 'drawing-office school' of fortification. His leading maxims were firstly to make the bastion flanks perpendicular to the rampart in all cases: to make their length one-sixth of the side of the polygon of the trace: and to make the 'gorge' of the bastion (the inside end, between the flanks) one-third of the side of the polygon. He insisted that the dimensions of the work be governed by the effective range of the contemporary musket, which he claimed to be 200 metres: from this he deduced that the maximum distance from the junction of flank and rampart of one bastion to the 'salient angle' (the outermost point) of its neighbour should not be

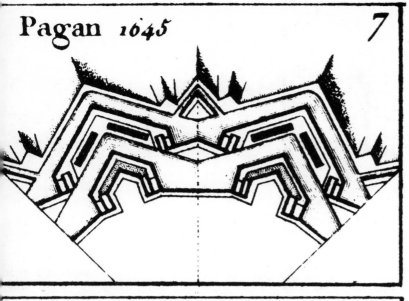

One of Pagan's designs using a double ditch system.

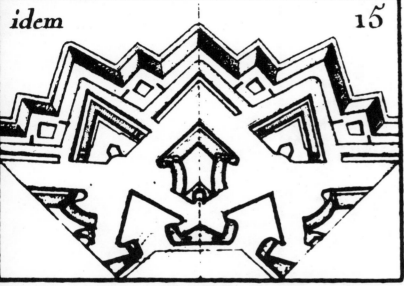

Another Pagan design using "detatched bastions"

A Cormontaign design using subsidiary external lines beyond the principal work.

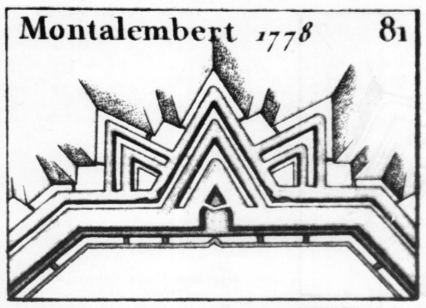

Montalembert *1778* **81**

idem **89**

Top and Centre:

Two examples of Montalembert's system of fortification, showing his ornate bastions and the use of counterguards

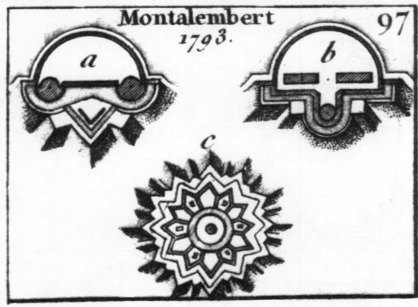

Montalembert *1793.* **97**

a   *b*

c

Montalembert's sketches for detached redoubts

One of the bastions of Blaye, on the Gironde. Built by Pagan, his peculiar rounded bastion ends can be seen here, as well as the deeply retired flanking battery. *Ian Hogg.*

more than 150 metres; and this line he christened the 'line of defence', an expression which remained in use for many years.

De Ville also took the Dutch fausse braye, the level strip between the rampart and the ditch, and developed it. In his writings this area took on a fresh importance as a catchment area into which the rampart might fall if bombarded, without the debris falling into the ditch and thus forming an aid for the assaulting party to cross by. But above all, de Ville moved in the opposite direction to Errard and began the move towards fortifying *outwards*; establishing the rampart as his principal defence line and then moving outwards to create further lines of defence and obstacles. On the far side of the ditch he established a wide pathway which became known as the 'chemin couvert' or 'covered way', running completely around the work. In front of this — 'towards the country' in engineer's parlance, as opposed to 'towards the place' — the earth was formed so as to produce a parapet and then sloped gradually down to the level of the surrounding ground so as to give a perfectly clear area around the work, known as the 'glacis', across which an enemy must advance in the face of the concentrated fire of the garrison. He also suggested the use of 'ravelins', small detached works within the ditch, guarding the ramparts, covering the ditch, flanking the bastions and covering the glacis.

Sixteen years after de Ville's work was published, it was eclipsed by the publication of *Les Fortifications du Comte de Pagan*, a masterly work by a man who had served at no less than twenty-five sieges to back up what he wrote. Blaise François, Comte de Pagan, had a spectacular military career: he enlisted at the age of 12; at 17 at the siege of Montauban in 1621 he was blinded in one eye by a musket shot; and while serving in Portugal as Quartermaster-General in 1642 he was blinded in the other eye. Thus, at the age of 38, he was forced to retire, having attained the rank of Marechal-de-Camp, and he died six years later. His book was, fortunately, finished before he lost his sight completely.

Pagan's major step was in his sequence of planning. His forerunners had laid out the interior of the fort to begin with, then surrounded it with a rampart, added bastions, and used the actual interior space as the controlling factor in their design. Pagan began by determining the best location for the bastions in relation to the terrain; he then joined these by ramparts and proceeded to work outwards, building a variety of protecting works in the ditch. He also settled the argument over the angle of the bastion's flank by making it at right-angles to the line of defence.

So far as is known the only work definitely and wholly attributable to Pagan is the fort at Blaye on the Gironde, which is today tolerably well preserved and contains within its walls a public camping ground. There is a slight possibility that during his service in Portugal he may have been concerned in fortification work there, but nothing is definite. Blaye, however, is remarkable in exhibiting several minor features of design which are not to be found in his treatise and which he doubtless abandoned as he progressed in experience. The bastions, for example, have peculiar rounded corners, some of which are built up into towers, while the flanks are perpendicular to the rampart. The ramparts themselves are stepped into two levels, giving the effect of an exceptionally wide chemin des rondes of the later form, though interrupted by the flanks of the bastions which spring from the upper level. In one or two cases the gorge of the bastion is closed by a peculiar turretted structure which gives the impression of a twelfth century castle planted on top of the rampart.

Plate XXX.

THE CITADEL.

Above: The citadel of Lille, as laid out by Vauban.

Right: Sebastien le Prestre de Vauban, 1633–1707. *Mansell Collection.*

Pagan's system introduces a more geometrical approach, a practice which had been gaining ground since de Ville's day. Three basic dimensions were laid down; the length of the external side of the polygon of the trace; the 'perpendicular'; and the length of the face of the bastion. The polygon is the figure described by joining the centres of the bastions; the perpendicular, in fortification, is the perpendicular to a line drawn between the salient angles of two adjacent bastions, and the dimension given is measured from the centre of this line inwards, so as to delineate the intersection of the lines of defence of that face. Given these dimensions, which Pagan tabulated for 'great, mean or little fortifications', the general dimensions and shape of the work were automatically determined, and from there on the dimen-

sions of the various features were fixed in proportion to the basic dimensions; we will look closer at this system of construction shortly. A feature of his designs (which can be well seen at Blaye) is the construction of 'orillons' — recessed sections in the flanks of the bastions intended to cover the face of the ramparts — which were half the length of the flanks. This was widely criticised at the time, but in fact it meant sufficient room in the orillons to mount at least four cannon to cover the ditch, and withal, these cannon were sufficiently recessed to be well protected from the front.

And eventually, in this procession of French practitioners, we come to Sebastien le Prestre de Vauban, the man whose name has become so inseparably connected with fortification that today it is the only one commonly known and the one to which anything remotely resembling a bastioned fort is immediately ascribed. Vauban did not invent the science of fortification, as we have already seen; indeed, very little in the way of constructional features can be definitely credited to him, but he brought together the various features and theories which had been thrown up in the previous hundred years and welded them into a coherent system.

Lille under siege during the Seven Years War. *National Army Museum.*

In some respects his enthusiasm carried him to excessive lengths; there was a certain amount of truth in the acerbic observation of Lord Sydenham, who spoke of 'Vauban and his school, in whose hands permanent fortification grew to be treated somewhat as a geometrical puzzle — a species of maze designed much on the principles which may have guided Henry's chief engineer in laying out the approaches to Fair Rosamunde's bower, and, on the whole, little more successful in keeping out the enemy.' Maréchal Marmont, in his memoirs, was also somewhat critical, saying that Vauban 'was more of an engineer than a general, and in making great numbers of fortresses he followed the bent of his own predilections.'

There is a good deal of truth in this; certainly Vauban appears to have tailored his fortification to his own tactical and strategical theories, which were not altogether sound. However, the point is that Vauban's far greater accomplishment has been obscured by his castle-building activities; he was the first man to bring some order to the business of sieges. He codified rules,

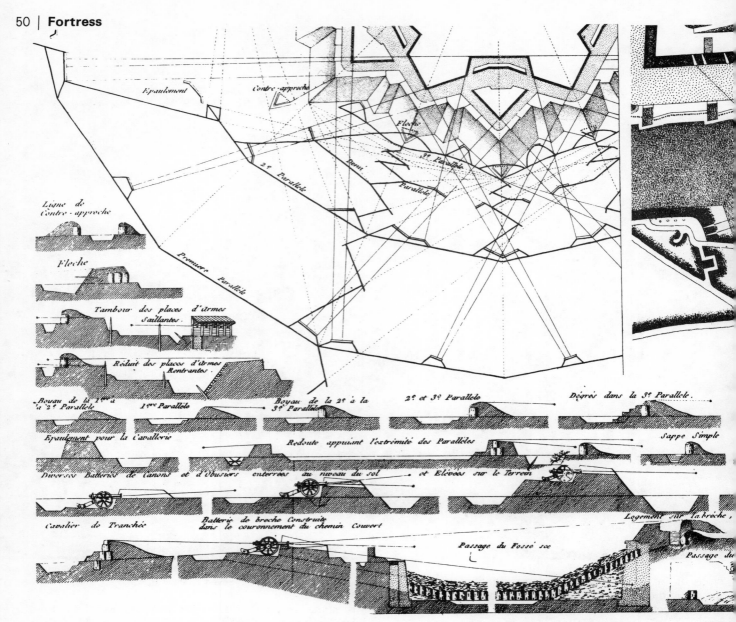

organised methods and systems, and reduced the business of laying siege to a defended place to a fine art. Indeed, on one or two occasions he actually conducted successful sieges against fortresses he had himself designed — an invidious position in which to find oneself: if the siege is a failure, you are blamed for it, and if it succeeds you are blamed for the poor quality of the defences.

Vauban, born in 1633, became a cadet in a cavalry regiment in 1651, and in 1652 was employed in the construction of fortifications at Clermont-en-Argonne, presumably in a fairly humble capacity. Shortly after this he was present at the siege of St Menehoud, so that within a short time of enlistment he had been exposed to both sides of the science he was to make his own. In the following year he was given a commission and placed in charge of repairing the fortifications of St Menehoud, after which he took charge of the siege of Clermont-en-Argonne — the first example of his involve-

ment in both sides of a siege — Landrécies, Conde and St Ghislain, all held at that time by the Spanish. In 1655 he was given the rank of 'Engineer-in-Ordinary to the King' and his course was set for the rest of his life.

Vauban's systems of fortification were largely governed by geometry, and we will investigate this aspect in the next chapter. What we might consider here is the other side of the battle, the matter of conducting a siege, and see how his introduction of organisation revitalised the whole business. Since the introduction of gunpowder there had been very little change in siege methods except for the substitution of cannon for engines. The attackers arranged themselves in a circle around the objective, to deny access to the besieged by supplies of food or reinforcements of troops. Artillery was brought up facing the walls at some selected point and opened fire at as short a range as possible in order to create and expand a breach in the wall. Once the breach was sufficiently large — a 'practicable breach' was the expression used —

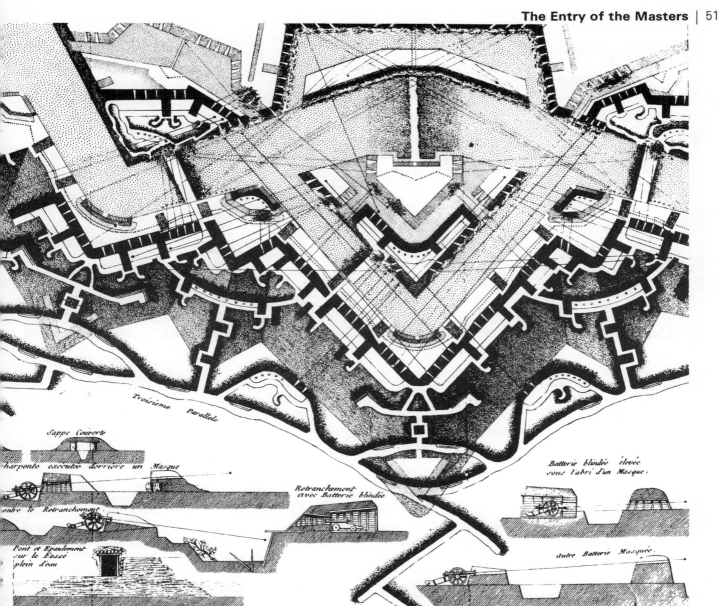

Troisième Parallèle

Sappe Couverte

Charpente executée derrière un Masque

Contre le Retranchement

Pont et Epaulement sur le Fossé plein d'eau

Retranchement avec Batterie blindée

Batterie blindée élevée sous l'abri d'un Masque.

autre Batterie Masquée.

Plates from Mandar's "De L'Architecture des Forteresses" of 1801 showing the science of siegecraft. The sections show various stages in the construction of the besieging lines and batteries

it was then rushed by infantry; success or failure depended on the vigour with which the assault was pressed home and the resolution with which it was resisted.

With the adoption of the mortar as a siege weapon, a new dimension was introduced; projectiles could be lobbed over the wall to do damage inside, depress the defender's spirits, wreck his stores and magazines and, of course, wreak havoc with the civil population in the hope that they might convince the defenders of the error of their ways and persuade them to surrender. But it was all very much a matter of individual inclination; the artillery battered away as it fancied, and the assault on the breach was generally an undisciplined rush with the object of being early into the place for the subsequent looting if one was lucky enough to survive the fight.

As musketry became a more common feature of the defence, such barefaced activities became more hazardous and it became necessary to protect the besieging batteries, usually by piling 'gabions', wickerwork baskets filled with earth, in front of the guns. Since the assault could not now cross the open country to attack the breach quite as easily as it had done in pre-musket days, the practice of trenching grew up, i.e. digging zig-zag trenches toward the intended breach, usually by night so that when the time for the assault came the troops had some cover for much of the distance. The trenches, as they advanced, were also screened by gabions, so their position and progress were no secret to the defenders, who were able to concentrate their attention on them and deal very severely with the

The siege of Schweidnitz, 1758, illustrating several features
of the contemporary siege. A mortar battery is on the left,
and its vertical fire appears to have started fires in the town.
On the right is a breaching battery protected by gabions and
breastworks. Between this battery and the town can be seen a
zig-zag sap full of soldiers. *John R. Freeman.*

assaulting force as it emerged. It is small wonder that
sieges under these conditions dragged on for many
weeks or months.

Vauban's objection to this performance was on the
grounds that it was wasteful; wasteful of lives, ammunition and, most of all, *time.* In 1673 at the siege of
Maastricht, he introduced the idea of excavating a
'parallel', a trench so-called since it was laid out parallel
to the faces of the work being attacked. The 'first
parallel' was cut at night, some 4–500 yards away from
the work, the earth being thrown up to form a parapet.
Before dawn, the trench was manned by the besiegers,
who then kept up covering small arms fire as necessary
while the excavation was widened and deepened, until
it eventually became a covered road. Bays were then
excavated and the siege guns brought along the parallel
and installed in these bays so that they could begin their
bombardment.

From the parallel, 'saps' or zig-zag trenches were cut
forward from numerous points to a convenient distance,
where they were halted and a fresh trench cut at right-
angles to the 'sap-head'; these trenches eventually
met the next sap and so a second parallel was formed.
This manoeuvre was repeated as necessary until the last
parallel was excavated in the glacis at the edge of the
ditch protecting the work.

With this final parallel established, it was then packed
with troops who would then rush out, clear the covered
way, cross the ditch by filling it with gabions or by the
use of ladders, and assault the work, using either a

breach blown by the artillery or simply by escalading.
The use of parallels and their parapet faces protected the
body of troops and guns; the zig-zag saps made forward
movement less hazardous; and since the parallels extended around the body of the place for a considerable
distance, the besieged force could never be certain of
where the attack was going to fall, particularly if an
escalade was contemplated or if the bombarding
artillery spread its efforts over three or four possible
breaching areas.

Although the 'sap and parallel' system sounds long
and laborious, it was in fact a good deal more rapid and
efficient than the earlier happy-go-lucky methods.
Vauban fairly proved this by taking Maastricht in
thirteen days, which was for that time an astonishing
feat, but one which he repeated at will in future sieges.
And it was at one of these, at Ath in 1696, that he introduced his other great innovation for overcoming
opposition: ricochet fire.

The term 'ricochet fire' is a little difficult to comprehend
today, conditioned as we are to rifled firearms and
elongated projectiles; the word 'ricochet' implies the
projectile bouncing off-course in random fashion, largely
governed by its spin, to an unpredictable distance.
Indeed, today the ricochet is looked upon as an unwanted
annoyance and the only time it is ever considered is when
laying out the boundaries of a firing range, when the
possibility of a projectile ricocheting has to be taken
into account. But in Vauban's terms it involved firing a
spherical shot from a smoothbore gun, over the rampart
from a flank, so as to enfilade the troops behind the
rampart, the ball skipping and bouncing along the
terreplein to dismount guns and disable men for a considerable distance. This principle was eagerly seized
upon, to the extent that it became a recognised tactic,
and the fortress engineer had to take steps to mitigate
its effects.

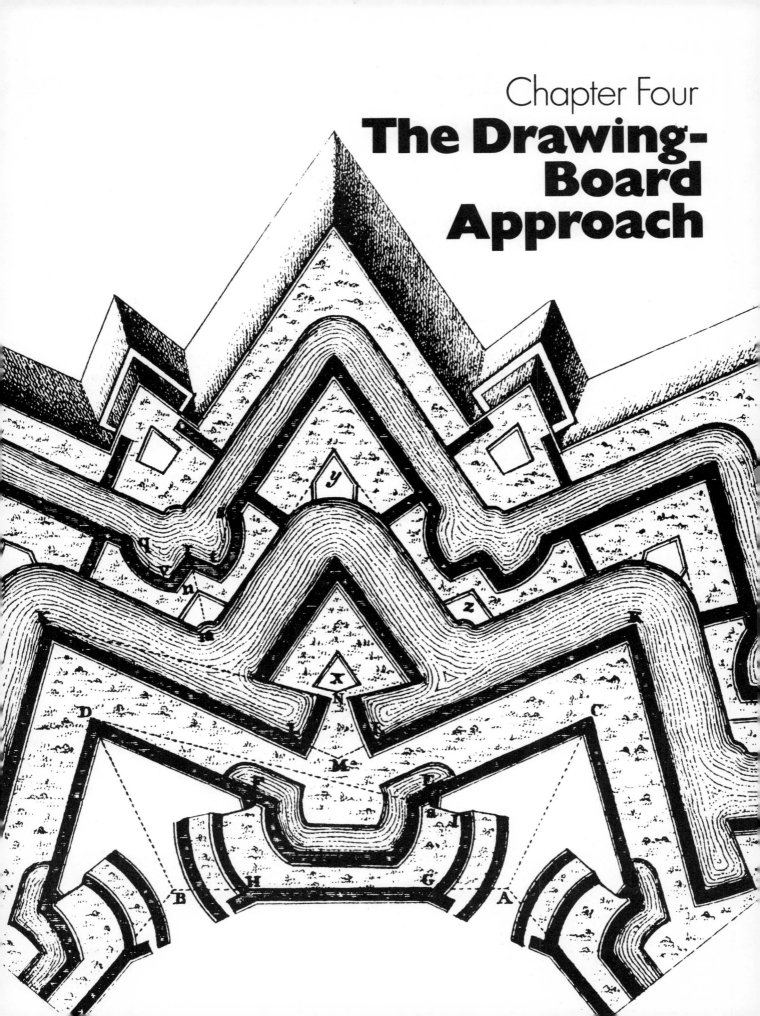

Chapter Four

The Drawing-Board Approach

Since the activities of the besieger were all aimed at crossing the ditch and assaulting the face on the inner side, it followed that the best method of bedevilling him was to allow him to expend his energy in capturing something relatively useless in the form of an extra work on the outside of the main work. Once having gained this, he was then faced with the prospect of crossing another ditch and assaulting another face, yet was poised in a place exposed to fire from the main work at short range and incapable of being protected by his own batteries. It is this relatively simple proposition which governed the complications of the fortification systems developed in the sixteenth and seventeenth centuries and brought to a fine pitch by Vauban. In order to see how everything fitted together, and to introduce some of the technicalities, we might now turn to an examination of Vauban's First System.

The first step in designing a work was to draw a polygon within which all the area to be defended could be contained, with as little wasted space as possible let us take, for example, a hexagon. The length of one side of this figure is a critical measure, since many other dimensions are evolved from it, and for this reason most engineers specified lengths of face for their different systems and tabulated them, together with the other derived measurements in order to save time and arithmetic. We will take one of Vauban's standards, '180 toises', a toise being a French unit of measurement equal to 6 English feet; or, in other words, a fathom. Converting this to a more convenient measure we have 360 yards. This is the distance between the tip (or salient angle or flanked angle — different engineers used different expressions) of one bastion to the same point on the adjacent bastion (A–B in Fig. 1).

This line is now bisected, and the perpendicular C–D drawn in, C being the point of intersection and D being set inwards by one-sixth of the distance A–B. This perpendicular is one of the basic tabulated dimensions,

and in order to achieve the correct outline its amount varies with the shape of the polygon: for hexagons and above, it is one-sixth of the side, for pentagons one-seventh, and for squares one-eighth.

The point D is now used to lay off the 'Lines of Defence' by drawing from A and B, and on each line a point (E and F) is set off at two-sevenths of the side to give the 'shoulders' of the bastion. The distance E–F is now set off from E on the line of defence to produce H, while the same distance set off from F on its line of defence gives G, and these two points mark the inward ends of the flanks of the bastion. Joining G and H now gives the line of the 'curtain' or rampart.

We can now, using the figure, define the following:
GEAKL is the bastion;
AE and AK are the faces of the bastion;
E is a shoulder of the bastion;
A is the salient angle or flanked angle of the bastion;
EG, FH, KL are the flanks of the bastion and
GL is the gorge of the bastion.

The result of all this is a 'Front of Fortification', and by repeating the process on each face the entire work is delineated. The line so drawn is the trace of the work and is the front face of the rampart. To trace the ditch, an arc of 40 yards is drawn from the tip of each bastion and a line drawn from the shoulders of the adjacent bastions so as to touch this arc; this form of construction ensuring that each section of ditch is adequately covered by a bastion flank.

The ditch was an excavation generally 15–30 feet deep, the earth from which went to form the parapet. The side of the ditch beneath the rampart is the 'escarp' while the opposite side is the 'counterscarp'. The ditch might be wet — i.e. filled with water — or dry, or in rare cases it was dry but capable of being rapidly filled with water from an adjacent river via sluices when necessary. The wet ditches, of course, gave the best protection —

Figure 1. A front of fortification, the basic figure of a bastioned work.

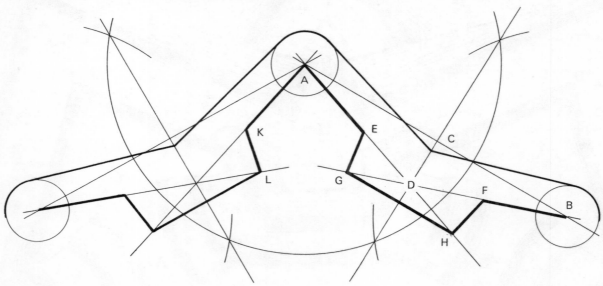

though when they were frozen hard they were less useful, as was found at the siege of Bergen-op-Zoom in 1814. But the number of bridges required in a large work, their maintenance and the problem of the precise moment to destroy them when a siege threatened led to the wet ditch's unpopularity; moreover it was a hazard to the health of the garrison if the water was static. The dry ditch was less of a problem, and it also gave a useful means of communication round the outside of the work, but it was less of an obstacle and there were numerous cases where the besiegers, once into the ditch, entrenched themselves there and took a good deal of evicting.

On the 'country' side of the ditch the ground was sloped away in the glacis, and the slope of the glacis was

Briancon, in the Hautes Alpes, one of Vauban's works. The bastioned enceinte of the town contains a citadel at the left. *French Government Tourist Office.*

a continuation of the slope of the upper part of the rampart so that it continued the line of fire from the rampart and prevented an attacker obtaining any cover from the fire. To provide a first line of defence the ditch edge of the glacis was cut away some 10 yards in front of the counterscarp to form a parapet, leaving the area between this and the counterscarp as the covered (or 'covert') way. Where the counterscarp was rounded, opposite the flanked angles of the bastions, the line of the glacis parapet continued until it was intersected by that of the adjacent face, and this enlarged portion of the covered

Figure 2. Vauban's curved flank or 'Orillon'.

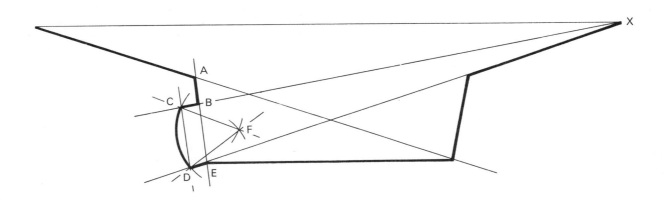

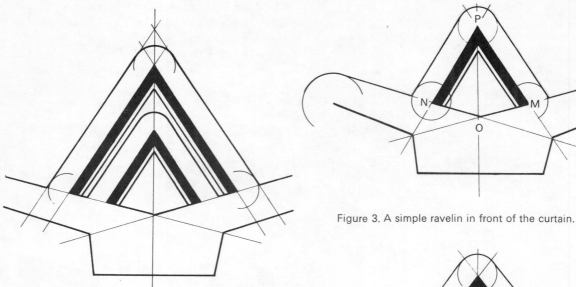

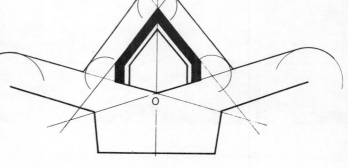

A redoubt in the ravelin, giving a second line of defence.

Figure 3. A simple ravelin in front of the curtain.

Figure 4. A ravelin with the addition of small flanks to allow better protection from the bastions.

way was known as a 'salient place of arms' since men could be gathered there for an assault or to clear the covered way if it were overrun by an enemy. Similar spaces, known as 're-entering places of arms' were set out at the angles of the counterscarp faces, and these could be used to give flank defence to sections of the covered way. A final improvement was due to the arrival of ricochet fire; 'traverses', banks of earth or masonry, were set at intervals across the covered way, recesses in the glacis allowing passage around them. These also had the advantage of chopping the covered way into small sections, and if an assault across the glacis gained one, the attackers could be easily confined within the section, since the passage in the glacis would only allow two men at a time to pass through, and they could be dealt with as they emerged.

With this as a basis, one commences to build. Firstly, the flanks of the bastions can be 'retired' to form 'orillons', by which means they are protected from observation and fire from the front but still retain their flanking function. Previous builders, such as Pagan, merely recessed a portion of the flank, but Vauban developed a refinement. The flank is divided into three (Fig. 2) and one-third laid off as AB. From the opposite bastion a line XB is drawn and prolonged by ten yards to give C. The line of defence XE is also drawn and prolonged ten yards to give D. C and D are now joined and used as the base of an equilateral triangle, from the apex F of which the arc delineating the orillon is struck; the portions of lines BC and DE intersected give the 'retired flanks' the curved section being the orillon.

Next we begin fortifying outwards, by constructing 'ravelins' (also known variously as 'half-moons' or 'demi-lunes'). There are outworks protecting the faces, and construction begins at the points 'O', where the counterscarp makes its re-entering angle in the centre of the face (Fig. 3). The perpendicular previously produced is extended to a point P, 110 yards in front of O, and from this point lines are drawn back to the shoulders of the bastions M and N. These give the 'flanks of the ravelin', and the gorge is plotted by using the line of the counterscarp. Now the ditch must be extended around the front of the ravelin, the width of this branch being 24 yards, set off by drawing an arc about P, setting off two points 24 yards from the ends of the flanks, and joining them. The work itself can be considered as an island in the ditch, the body being of the same height as the covered way and the flanks being given a parapet of the same height as the glacis; the gorge is left open, being provided with stairways ('pas de souris') giving access from the ditch. Some constructors preferred to place a second ravelin within the ravelin, as it were, calling this the 'redoubt in the ravelin', while others fashioned the ravelin with small flanks (Fig. 4).

The ravelin became a most important unit; its use dates from the early Italian engineers and it was brought to prominence by Speckel, a German engineer who

Figure 6. Below: A ravelin further protected by a bonette and two lunettes.

Figure 5. Tenailles; various forms of tenaille to protect the curtain and flank the ditch, also giving cover to parties who can move to clear the ditch in an assault.

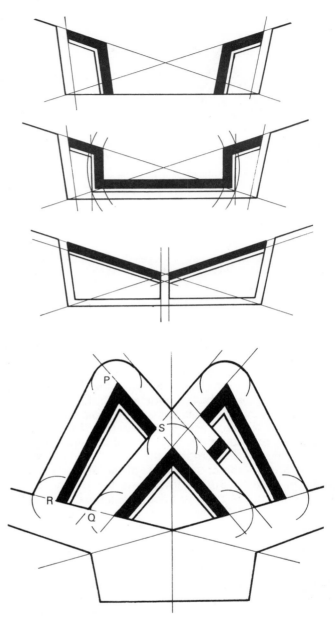

fortified Ulm, Colmar and Basel. The object of the ravelin is to cover the curtain and the flank of the bastion as well as to create an additional obstacle before the main work.

The next refinement is the 'tenaille', a small work or combination of works in the ditch in front of the curtain, set low so that its parapet is some 2 or 3 feet higher than the body of the ravelin. It can thus fire into the ravelin, should that work be taken: it also covers the ditch between the ravelin and the redoubt in the ravelin if one is built; and it covers the main ditch at a lower level than the orillons. Vauban recognised three types of tenaille, shown in Fig. 5, but there is no need to enter into the question of their precise dimensions. An additional useful feature of these tenailles is that the space behind them, in a dry ditch, becomes a protected area in which troops could be formed up for counter-attacking any enemy who had gained the ditch; to allow such troops to assemble, a postern gate was often cut in the escarp, connecting with the body of the place by a tunnel, and the tenailles protected and concealed this gate.

The ravelin can be further strengthened, and its utility as an obstacle increased, by building 'lunettes' and 'bonnettes' (Fig. 6). The lunettes are constructed by bisecting the face of the ravelin and setting off 60 yards from the counterscarp of the ravelin ditch to give one face. The rear face is the line of the counterscarp of the main ditch, while the outline is completed by setting off 50 yards along the counterscarp of the main ditch. A subsidiary ditch, 24 yards wide, then surrounds the lunette: a similar work is built on the other face of the ravelin. The bonnette covers the flanked angle of the ravelin; it may be likened to an additional ravelin, its rear face being on the line of the counterscarp and its

Figure 7. Tenaillons; the one on the right has a recessed battery which protects the ditch but which cannot be flanked.

faces being produced by bisecting the face of the lunettes. The ditch in front is 20 yards wide. There are, of course, other dimensions possible; Vauban also designed lunettes which were two-thirds of the face of the ravelin and had narrower gorges.

Not only did these outworks protect the ravelin and confuse the attacker, but they formed a self-supporting community of defence, since it meant that four separate works, all defended and ditched, had to be taken by the assault before the area could be put to any use; it was of little avail for an enemy to capture, say, one

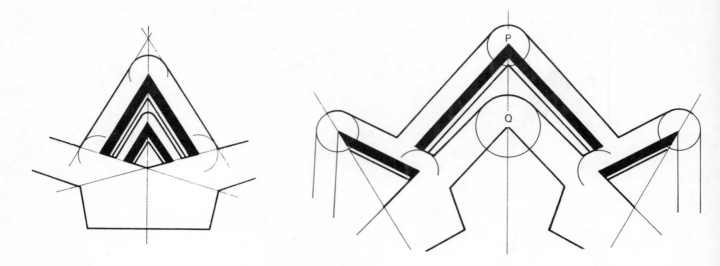

Figure 8. A counterguard before a ravelin, simply a larger version of a ravelin with a redoubt and giving one more mass of masonry to confound the attacker.

Figure 9. A counterguard before a bastion.

lunette, since that was open to being raked with fire by the force in the ravelin and the tenaille. Notice also that capturing inwards means that no work to the rear, to the place, is ever exposed to danger from the outworks which have been captured; for example, an enemy in the bonnette could do no significant damage to the lunettes or ravelin due to their parapets, while the defences have the entire centre of the bonnette at their mercy.

Another variant of this system of protection for the ravelin was to construct 'tenaillons' (Fig. 7.). These are plotted by extending the faces of the ravelin across the ditch for 60 yards to produce the line SP, and measuring 30 yards along the counterscarp of the main ditch from Q to R. Joining SPQR now gives the outline of the tenaillon, and the 24-yard ditch is extended around the front. Various refinements are possible: retiring one section of the face to conceal a battery, for example, or throwing a central ditch and parapet across the body of the work in order to 'retrench' it, giving a second line of defence should the parapet be overcome. A point to be noted here is that where tenaillons are required the depth of the ravelin must be less than the normal 110 yards, otherwise the salient angles of the tenaillons become too acute to be practically defensible.

Another method of defending the ravelin is by use of the 'counterguard' (Fig. 8), which might best be described as a bonnette pulled down over the ears of the ravelin. It performs most of the functions of lunettes and bonnettes and it also serves to conceal the ravelin from the besiegers: thus having assaulted and gained the counterguard, they would find themselves in possession of a thin piece of architecture, 20 yards wide of which the parapet took up 6 yards, with another ditch in front and an angry ravelin across it.

However, counterguards were more favoured in front of the bastion itself: the self-supporting complex of ravelin, lunette and bonnette formed a very sound

unit, but so far nothing has been done about additional protection for the bastion, and the counterguard is one of the few methods applicable. When placed in front of the bastion (Fig. 9) its rear face is based on the counterscarp wall, its salient angle (P) is 150 yards from the salient angle of the bastion (Q) and its width at its extremities 30 yards: the usual 24-yard ditch was then run in front.

Let us pause here and contemplate what has been wrought so far by producing a drawing of a portion of a polygon protected by the various outworks described, together with a section through them (Figs. 10 and 11). It is obvious that any attacker ill-advised enough to attempt an assault from B to A would have to overcome the glacis and covered way and then cross five ditches and take four outworks before arriving at the escarp wall of the main work. (It will be appreciated that for the sake of delineating the relative position, the tenaille has been included in the section, a slight draughtsman's licence.) Moreover the interlocking defence of the ravelin complex would be a formidable obstacle in itself. Notice also that ricochet fire aimed at clearing the rampart of any face of one work cannot endanger any other work in enfilade. On paper, perhaps, all this looks simple, but when met face to face on the ground the proliferation of masonry, the branching ditches, and the careful planning so that from no point is it possible to see exactly how many lines of defence confront one, the prospect is impressive and daunting. Even without the hazard of being shot at, it takes considerable time and energy to scramble about a work in the present day in order to try and discern what the various arrangements are, even with a plan or aerial photograph to guide one.

But M. Vauban and his contemporaries were by no means satisfied at this stage of the design; we can go back to Lord Sydenham once more for a summary of the system. 'Draw a polygon round the area to be defended;

Figure 10. A front of fortification completed by the addition of the various features so far discussed

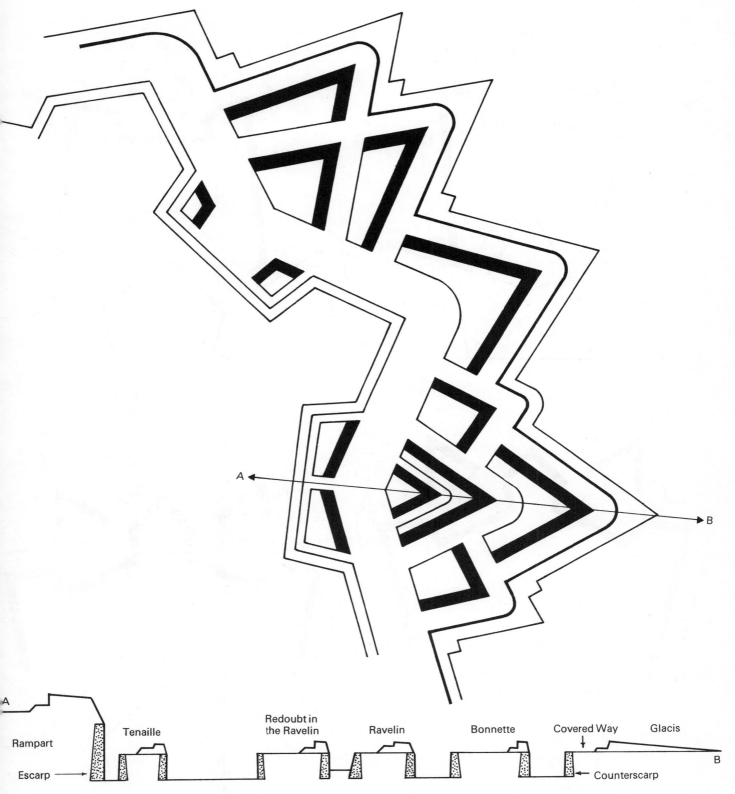

Figure 11. A section on the line A-B of the previous figure, to show how the various components conceal and reinforce each other

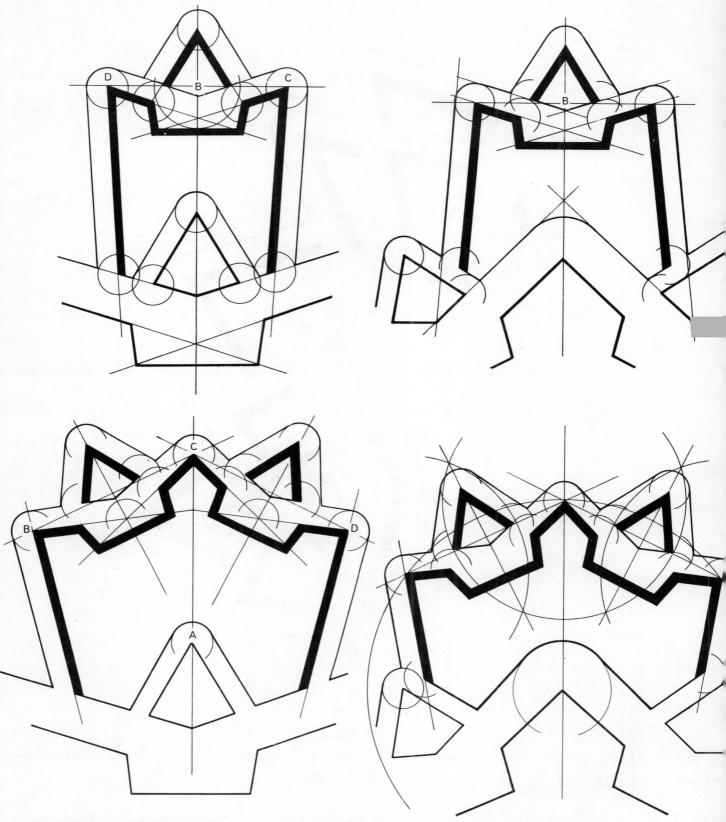

Figure 12. A hornwork before a curtain and ravelin

Figure 13. A hornwork before a bastion

Figure 14. A crownwork before a ravelin

Figure 15. A crownwork before a bastion

make of each side a bastioned front, obtain saliency and crossfire over the front by ravelins . . . supplement this trace by any number of counterguards, place an independent réduit in every available angle; build high cavaliers to give simultaneous lines of fire; retrench everything retrenchable; throw out hornworks, crownworks, tenailles, demi-tenaillons and what-not to the front, thus infinitely increasing the geometrical possibilities; finally build a citadel in which most of the above artifices can be repeated inside the main line, and one arrives at a fair idea of what may be termed the linear method of fortification.' He was, of course, being sarcastic once again about 'Vauban and his school', but nevertheless it was a fairly accurate description. But cavaliers? hornworks? crownworks? Let us now move into somewhat deeper water.

A 'cavalier' we can dismiss fairly rapidly, since it was a less common feature; the term denotes an additional raised work within the body of the place, erected in order to obtain *command* (i.e. the advantage of height) over its surroundings. Cavaliers could be erected in bastions, in which case they generally followed the polygonal shape of the bastion, or on the curtain, in which case they were generally semi-circular. But the only reason for having a cavalier was if the neighbourhood of the work had a rise of ground in such a position as to command some part of the defences; the cavalier was then built to overtop this rise and give additional fire-power. As the passage quoted above suggests, cavaliers also permitted an augmentation of the fire-power by providing an additional layer of musketry or cannon, but their employment for this purpose alone was seldom justified.

'Hornworks' and 'crownworks' are almost identical, the difference often being hard to detect without a plan and, moreover, the terms have come to be applied fairly loosely, so that some large outworks which do not fit the precise definitions are called hornworks in default of any better term having been coined. Strictly speaking a hornwork is 'an outwork composed of two half-bastions and a curtain, with two long sides.' When it is placed before the curtain, it is laid out by plotting a point B 160 yards in front of the salient angle of the ravelin (Fig. 12). From here a line at right-angles is developed, marking two points C and D at 110 yards to each side. From these two points a front of fortification is developed in the same way as was done for the main body of the work, making the perpendicular 36 yards and the faces 60 yards. From C and D the flanks are drawn so as to terminate on the faces of the bastions, 10 yards from the shoulders. The usual 24-yard ditch surrounds the hornwork, which is then completed by a ravelin 70 yards deep whose faces are aligned on the shoulders of the hornwork's half-bastions.

When built before a bastion, the shape differs very slightly. The construction point B is 200 yards in front of the flanked angle, and the flanks are aligned on points 10 yards inwards from the ditch on the faces of the adjacent ravelins, a construction which makes the base of the work somewhat wider than before (Fig. 13).

The crownwork is a much larger affair, much less common, and can be likened to a hornwork expanded so as to include a bastion on its front. This means, of course, that the face contains two fronts of fortification, and this opens up the possibility of adding two ravelins, or, indeed, extending the ramifications of ravelin, tenaillon

Figure 16. Left: An arrow, a salient outwork reached through the glacis.

Figure 17. Below right: A detached redoubt, reached from the covered way.

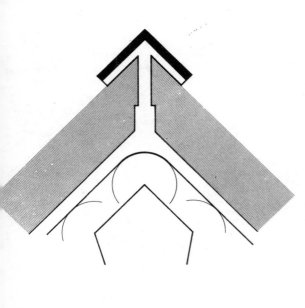
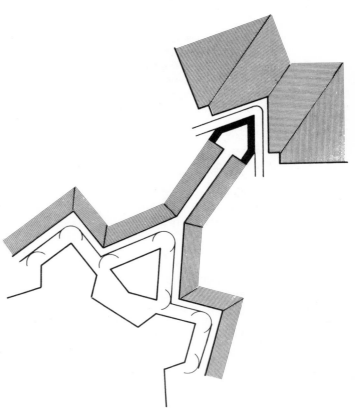

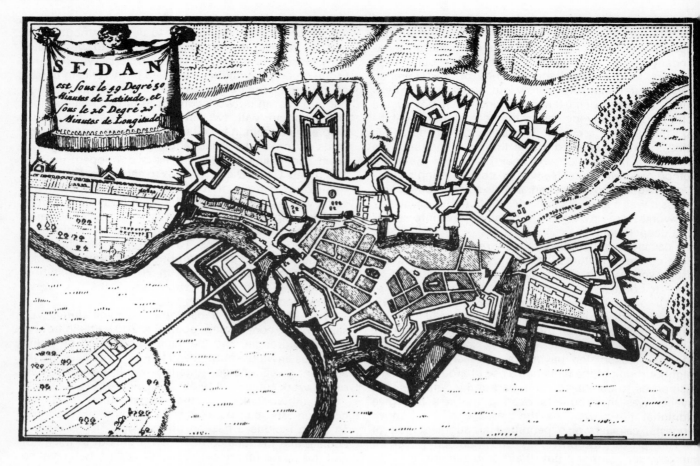

and bonnette as far as one cares to go. A crownwork before a ravelin (Fig. 14) starts with plotting the tip of the crownwork bastion C at 240 yards from the tip of the ravelin. An arc is then drawn about C and chords of 220 yards plotted to give the angles of the half-bastions B and D. Using this as a basis the two fronts are constructed using the same 36-yard perpendicular and 60-yard faces as was done with the hornwork. The flanks are then produced from B and D to terminate in the bastions of the main work 50 yards from their shoulders. Ravelins are then added, again using the same dimensions as for those of the hornwork.

When constructed in front of a bastion, the 240-yard arc is drawn from the flanked angle of the bastion, after which construction continues in the same way as before, the flanks being terminated on the adjacent ravelins, 50 yards in from the ditch (Fig. 15).

One very obvious thing about these works is that they are going to be an expensive item both to build and to man and arm, and for that reason neither was exactly common. Their principal purpose seems to have been to occupy a piece of ground which otherwise might prove useful to the enemy or to cover the entrance to a town or work, or to form a bridgehead, in which cases a gate would be formed in the forward face. Another purpose quoted by contemporary writers was to place hospitals, stores and barracks inside them, to act as a sort of suburb or overflow to the body of the work, but there seems to be

Above: Plan of Sedan, c. 1700, showing the use of hornworks

Opposite page: The spur bastion at Dover Castle; this was originally built as an earthwork in the 13th century, the brickwork being added in Napoleonic times. *Mike Jarvis.*

The citadel at Tournai, Belgium. Notice that at A and B a river passes through the glacis to feed the wet ditch.

an element of ambiguity here; one cannot be certain whether the hornwork was intended to take the stores or whether the stores were put in the hornwork in order to take advantage of the space available. There is a form of Parkinson's Law in military quartering which says that troops and their ancillaries will always expand to fill whatever room is available to them.

Vauban, however, seems to have been highly taken with hornworks and crownworks, notably in his defences of Tournai, Ypres and Strasbourg; so much so that one eighteenth century critic observed that it seemed likely that his purpose was more to terrify the enemy than to actually strengthen the defence. Strasbourg had five large hornworks, one of which was additionally decorated with tenaillons at each flank and bonnettes covering each half-bastion.

A minor advanced work, though rarely used, was the 'arrow'; built into the glacis, it was to all intents and purposes a sort of detached ravelin connected to the covered way by a passage (Fig. 16). Even more ornate and uncommon is the 'detached redoubt' (Fig. 17) which was a larger species of ravelin placed some distance from the work and connected by a covered way flanked by earth parapets piled so as to form an extension of the glacis. It had its own ditch, covered way and glacis, and since the covered way is also at the level of the surrounding ground and exposed at its flanks one cannot credit the construction with much resisting power. Moreover there was always considerable risk of the enemy cutting the covered way and taking the redoubt in reverse, a manoeuvre which also gave access to the covered way of the main ditch. Although works with detached redoubts can still be found (there is an excellent specimen at Fort Burgoyne in Dover), they are usually rather better constructed than this example of Vauban's design, and I rather suspect that this was one of his paper exercises.

To further extend the defence, confuse the enemy, and add to the expense, Vauban advocated that where water was available, a second ditch could now be excavated in front of the glacis of the main ditch. This was then to be provided with ravelins at the re-entering angles of the glacis, so that they fell opposite to the faces of the bastions of the main work.

This, then, was Vauban's First System; and apart from the proportions of the basic polygon and the curved flanks of the bastions, none of it was of his own invention, every one of the various outworks having been devised and described previous to his adopting them. Nevertheless he deserves credit for welding all the ideas into a homologous whole, and certainly the result was a sound defensive work for its day. The only serious criticism ever levelled at the system was the flanks of the bastions were rather short, so that there was insufficient room to mount many guns, and an enemy battery of superior strength could defeat them, but this rather overlooks the masking

effect of most of the outworks. Certainly Vauban was sufficiently confident of its strength to use the system in fortifying Lille, Saarlouis and many other towns.

Vauban later developed the designs known as his Second and Third Systems; these were not so much improvements on his First, as might be supposed, but modifications to suit particular cases. His Second System (Fig. 18) was developed in order to adapt the principles of his First System to the strengthening and improvement of a work already in existence, while his Third System (Fig. 19) was only a slight improvement on his Second. It was for his Second System that he invented his 'Tower Bastion', a device peculiarly his own. These were joined to the original wall to give the desired bastion effect and were of two tiers, the lower being a central magazine surrounded by casemates covering the ditch to the flanks, the upper being a roof platform with embrasures for guns and a substantial masonry traverse in the centre to protect at least half the occupants from ricochet fire. An interesting refinement is the division of the casemate section into individual bays, with embrasures in the dividing walls, so that should the tower be entered by an enemy the assault could be if not entirely contained, at least conveniently channelled and considerably delayed. He was also careful to include ventilating flues to try and clear the smoke from the casemates, though from contemporary reports it seems to have had little effect.

A section drawn through the First System (Fig. 20) will allow us to complete our cataloguing of the various

Left: View of the Spur bastion, Dover from the Castle. *Mike Jarvis*

Figure 18. Left: Vauban's Second System

Figure 19. Below: Vauban's Third System

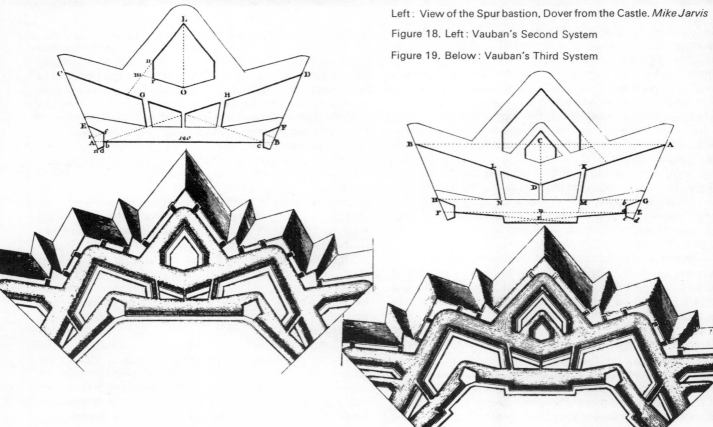

features of contemporary fortification and also to deal with the remaining technical terms of the day. Commencing in the centre of the body of the place, the area at the level of the surrounding country is taken as the datum; the height of any component over this is its *command*. In the rear of the rampart is firstly a raised section of fairly considerable width, the 'terreplein', upon which cannon could be mounted. Then comes the 'banquette' or fire-step on which the soldiers stood in order to fire small arms across the parapet, which is the highest point of the rampart. From the crest of the parapet the rampart runs in two stages, one, the 'superior slope', forming the upper surface, and the other, the 'exterior slope', being the outward surface. The exterior slope runs down to the level of the datum, whereupon the ditch commences. In some constructions there was a space between the foot of the exterior slope and the inner edge of the ditch (the escarp) known as the 'berm' and primarily intended to catch any earth dislodged from the rampart by bombardment and to prevent it falling into the ditch.

The escarp wall of the ditch was often topped with a 'cordon', a layer of masonry protruding from the face to make things more difficult for an escalading party. In the ditch were the various outworks, and the front edge of the ditch was revetted by the counterscarp wall. Then comes the covered way and the glacis, and it is worth noting that the slope of the glacis is an extension of the slope of the superior slope of the rampart, so that the whole of the glacis is open to fire from the parapet on the rampart. At the foot of the glacis it was common practice to place a variety of obstacles: felled trees with their branches facing the enemy were a favoured item, known as 'abattis'. In addition, 'trous de loup', deep pits containing sharpened stakes, were scattered about this area, it being mandatory that they be at least 6 feet deep in order to be too deep to be adapted by an enemy as firing pits for musketry. Finally an 'advanced glacis' might be built, although there seems little good reason for doing so.

Vauban is estimated to have fortified, either completely or partially, anything between 92 and 150 places; the exact figure is in doubt, though the lower estimate

seems the more likely. As already indicated, any bastioned work in France or the Low Countries, and sometimes even further afield, is likely to be attributed to Vauban. But there were other engineers who adopted some of the features of his system, and, of course, there were engineers who elected to go their own way; and in many cases their departure from Vauban's doctrines is hard to detect on the ground, requiring an accurate plan before the differences can be fully appreciated. With few exceptions though, most of them went to a degree of elaboration which was impractical — certainly in their published plans — and departed from Vauban's relatively simple tenets. Although it is notable that while many engineers published splendid 'Atlasses' of ornate and complicated systems, when it came down to actually building a fortification they generally preferred something a good deal more utilitarian.

One such was M. Minno, Baron de Coehorn, a General of Artillery who later changed hats and became a Lieutenant-General of Infantry and, later still, became Director-General of Fortifications in Holland. He was a contemporary of Vauban, to the extent that they came face-to-face when Vauban laid siege to Namur in 1692. Vauban proceeded with his saps and parallels, and threatened the town from several points at once, placing the garrison in a considerable dilemma. He eventually took the place after a thirty-day siege, and Racine, who was present as the King's official historian, recorded that when Vauban and Coehorn met, the Dutchman was somewhat disgruntled at Vauban's many-pronged system of attack. Had the assault been made in the proper form, Coehorn complained, the town would have held out for another fortnight at least.

Coehorn published his systems of fortification some years before he became much concerned with the actual construction of works, and what he actually built turned out to be a good deal more simple than what he had proposed on paper. However, it must be borne in mind that Coehorn's field of activity was in the Low Countries where it was impossible to excavate for more than 4 feet without coming to water, and where water and swampy ground were commonplace items which could be turned to useful account. He was, moreover, a

Figure 20. A cross-section of a simple fort developed on Vauban's method, showing the various features and the technical terms

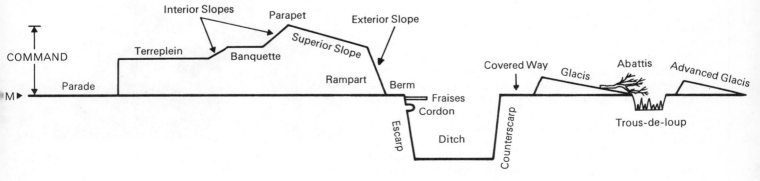

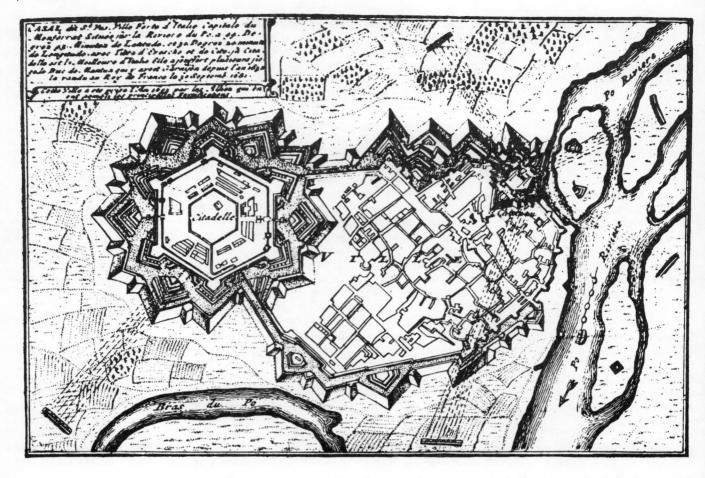

thoroughly experienced artilleryman and a soldier with a wide knowledge of the other aspects of battle beyond the siege, a general military experience much greater than that of Vauban, and his designs reflect the conviction that no matter how well a rampart was built, it would eventually succumb to bombardment by heavy artillery. For that reason his designs were intended to place such a series of obstacles in front of an attacker that actually reaching the rampart would be extremely difficult and hazardous.

As an example of the extremes of Coehorn's theories, we might illustrate his Second System (Fig. 21). There are two 'arrowhead' bastions with large flanks, bearing gun batteries at two levels; these flanks, and the intervening curtains are protected by small wet ditches with parapets behind, acting as tenailles. Before the bastions and ditches is a wide dry ditch connected to a ravelin which contains a redoubt, and this is surrounded by a 48-yard wide wet ditch. Beyond this comes the 'second counterscarp', with a parapet at its front, traversed and provided with redoubts at every angle. Then comes another wet ditch of 28 yards width and a wide covered way with redoubts and traverses, and 'coffers' or breastworks built into the re-entering angles of the glacis.

The obvious feature of all this is its enormous depth from 'place' to 'country'; the salient angle of the ravelin

Casal, Italy, in the 17th century; an example of a 'star' fort with a bastioned citadel inside. The enceinte of the town is a peculiar cross between bastioned and star influence, with small square towers at the bastion flanks.

Minno, Baron von Coehorn, 1641–1704. *Radio Times Hulton Picture Library*

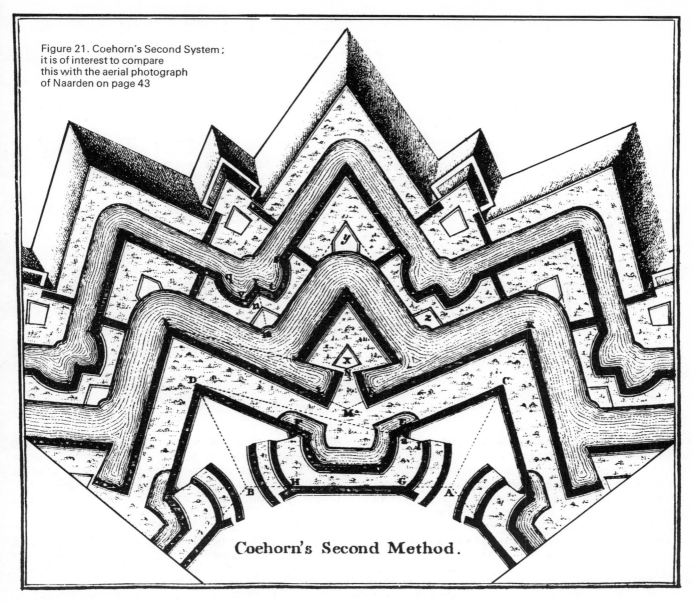

Figure 21. Coehorn's Second System; it is of interest to compare this with the aerial photograph of Naarden on page 43

Coehorn's Second Method.

is 250 yards from the curtain, and the salient angle of the covered way as much again. While any conceivable line of attack is flanked from several directions and extremely hazardous, the whole proposition is prone to collapse under its own weight; if one cares to plot the whole work — it is a heptagon founded on a side of 252 yards — it will be found that the area of ground absorbed by the defences is five times the area within the body of the place, which leads one to wonder whether the place could ever have accommodated sufficient troops to man the defences of all the various works and outworks. Whether this, or the undoubted vast expense of construction, was the deciding factor, we do not know, but when Coehorn came to actually building, his planning was but little removed from Vauban's First System, as the plans of Bergen-op-Zoom (generally taken as being Coehorn's masterpiece) will show.

Nevertheless, Coehorn's plans reveal some interesting features; a notable item is his 'couvre-face', a very thin counterguard used with his first system and intended to protect the body of the place until the siege was well advanced. Another innovation was the use of reverse fire to protect his dry ditches. The rampart at the edge of the wet ditch had a masonry gallery in its rear face, beneath the banquette, into which the defenders could retire when the rampart was overrun. This gallery had loopholes facing into the dry ditch, so that any enemy who gained the ditch would be under fire from these 'counterscarp galleries' as well as from the flanks of the bastions and the tenailles. A further point is that Coehorn arranged his dry ditches to be excavated about 4 feet below the datum, thus forestalling any possibility of an enemy attempting to entrench himself in the dry ditch — one spade's depth and the digger was into the water table.

The Modern, French, or Improved System.
Principal features include a cavalier in the bastion, a redoubt in
the re-entering place of arms, and caponiers leading from the
tenaille to the redoubt in the ravelin.

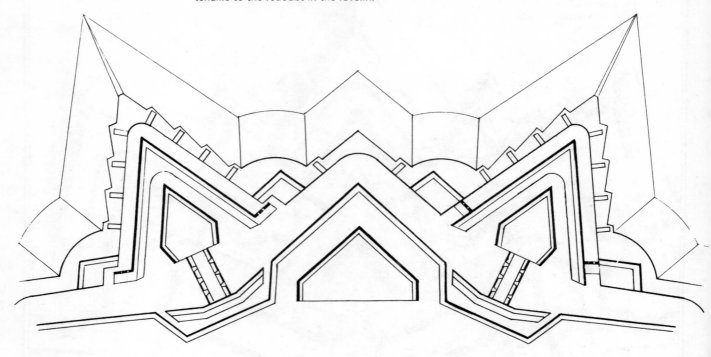

The works of Vauban and Coehorn were well wrought and stayed serviceable for many years. But there was no lack of engineers willing to try and improve on them, even if only on paper, and the eighteenth century saw numerous 'Systems of Fortifications' published, notably in France, where the engineers appear to have convinced themselves, and much of Europe, that they were the sole fountain of knowledge on the subject. When one comes to examine their propositions it is difficult, at first sight, to see where they differ from Vauban or Coehorn, and even when the difference is explained, it is often no more clear. The system attributed to Cormontaigne, for example appears at first glance to differ little from Vauban's First System. The distinction, on close examination, lies in the faces of the bastions being two-sevenths of the side of the polygon instead of one-sixth, the ravelins being much deeper, and their flanks directed at a point well along the face of the bastion. This leads to a slightly better covering by the ravelin, space to build a bigger redoubt inside it, and shorter curtains. An innovation of Cormontaigne's was the 'line of crémaillère' in the parapet of the covered way, allied with traverses, which allowed the traverse to be better defended in the event of the covered way being invaded.

Vauban never published his systems, but in 1729, after his death, they were produced in print by a M. Belidor, Professor of Mathematics at the French Artillery School. Belidor was honest enough to reproduce Vauban's work exactly, but he was no more capable of resisting the urge to embellish than was any other fortification expert of the time. His 'System' revolved around turning the bastions into detached and fragmented units, since an objection frequently voiced was that a single breach in a bastion usually led to the capitulation of the garrison. Belidor's First System (Fig. 23) was quite a sound design; he then ornamented it into a Second System and a Third System, both of which were little short of being mathematicians' delights and, like Coehorn's theoretical figures, highly unlikely to be acceptable in practice however powerful their defensive capabilities might promise to be.

In about 1750 the French engineer's school at Mézières produced a refinement upon Vauban which was for some years known as the 'Mézières System'. This was later improved by General Noizet into the 'Modern French System' which was to remain the accepted standard for as long as bastioned fortification existed, being held up as the ultimate in design as late as the 1870's, although, in fact, few works were ever built to it. The modern system was little changed from Vauban or Cormontaigne, though some thought had been given to improvements in the power of artillery. A cavalier was placed in the bastion in order to increase fire-power, while the ditch before the ravelin was crossed by a 'caponier' or protected passage, the structure of which served to mask the lower portion of the bastion from battering fire directed from a possible position on the glacis at the end of the ditch. This was later, under Noizet, improved by building a deliberate 'mask' across the ditch line, dog-legging the ditch around it; such an

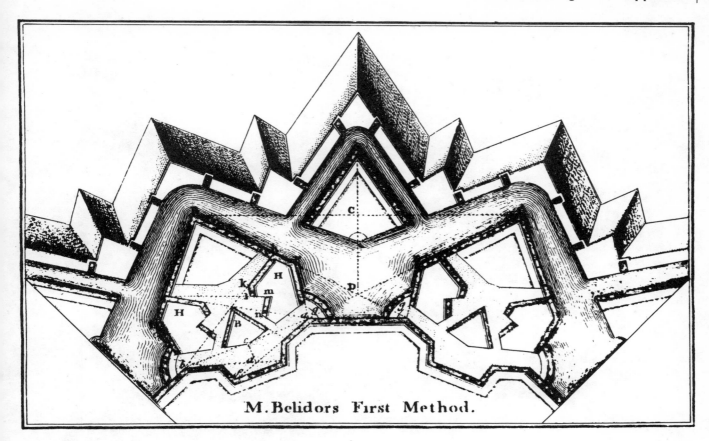

M. Belidors First Method.

arrangement protected the bastion passively by inter-posing a barrier and actively since it now served to mount a battery which could deal with any attempt to lodge in the glacis crest before it had a chance of success.

Among the last practitioners of the bastioned school of building were Haxo and Choumara, both comman-dants of engineers in their time. Haxo's principal innovation, which was later widely adopted in England, was his 'Haxo Casemate' formed in the parapet of the work, arched with masonry, and then covered with earth. The casemates were open at the rear to the terreplein, so as to reduce the usual smoke problem by allowing ample ventilation and also to allow guns to be run in and out easily. In English works they usually became single mounded casemates on the ramparts, their front faces merged into the parapet, though in rare instances — Laira Battery at Plymouth is one — groups of three casemates, connected by cross passages and mounded into the rampart were used.

Haxo apparently never published any of his designs, being on record as having opined that systems were merely an exhibition of principles, not rules to be slavishly followed. Choumara, however, produced a 'Mémoires sur la Fortification' in 1847, though much of his theory was, according to contemporary critics, based on Haxo's teachings. The most interesting of Choumara's suggestions (there is no evidence of any work being built according to his recommended system) lay in his

Figure 23. Belidor's First Method, an ornate system which saw little practical application

subterranean arrangements.

The mine had remained a factor in siege warfare, though now, of course, it was an explosive mine rather than a mine of subsidence. The tunnel would be driven, sacks or barrels of gunpowder placed, and at a suitable time the charge would be exploded under the work. (Coehorn and the Dutch school, of course, regarded the mine with some amusement, since they were in no danger of having it used in their area of activity.) As a result, the practice had grown up of driving 'countermines' beneath the work, sometimes running far out beneath the ditch and glacis. These galleries were quite substan-tial works, some 6 feet high and 3 feet wide tunnels, lined and arched in brick; and during a siege they would be patrolled by sharp-eared miners alert for sounds of enemy activity. When such activity was detected, a short tunnel could rapidly be cut from the nearest gallery until it was close to the approaching mine; the countermine tunnel was then packed with gunpowder and blocked off with earth to try and contain the explosion, and fired while the enemy miners were at work, in the hope of destroying them and their mine.

Choumara carried this idea further by advocating massive vaulted galleries 16 to 20 feet wide, running out for several hundred yards before the glacis. Six of these would be driven from each front and linked at

Dover Castle; a ditch constructed in Napoleonic times with escarp and counterscarp walls, the ramparts on the right and the glacis of the work on the left. *Mike Jarvis*

intervals by cross-galleries. The immense labour entailed in such a plan can be imagined; moreover one cannot help thinking that such subterranean highways would constitute a foolproof method of attack should an enemy mine inadvertently strike one — as would seem highly likely from their proposed density.

It might be pointed out in passing that these counter-mine galleries, together with passages beneath ditches to give access to ravelins and counterguards, are the explanation of many of the mysterious tunnels found in the lower levels of old works. Today they are invariably choked with rubbish or sealed by a roof fall, and they are usually explained away as being a connection to some adjacent work, be it ever so far away. I have been assured that tunnels beneath Crown Hill Fort at Plymouth were connected with the Citadel, some three and a half miles away, and also that the Citadel itself was connected by a tunnel to Drake's Island Battery, two miles away in the middle of Plymouth Sound. These mythical tunnels are on a par with those usually reputed to run from ruined monasteries to the nearest nunnery.

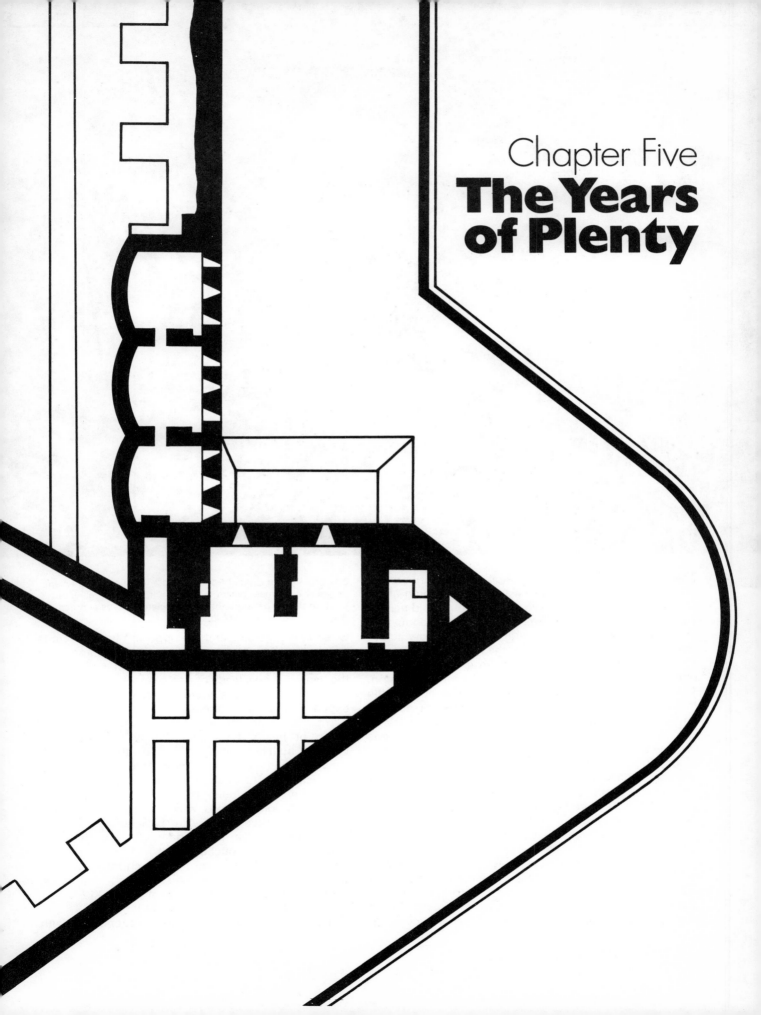

Chapter Five
The Years of Plenty

The Storming of Cuidad Rodrigo, 1812. The lack of sufficient engineer equipment meant that Wellington had to rely more upon dash and gallantry than upon scientific saps and parallels. *National Army Museum.*

The War of the Spanish Succession, when Marlborough changed the map of Europe, was a wide-ranging affair, producing battles which have become household names. But in addition to Blenheim, Ramillies, Malplaquet and Oudenarde, there was considerable ebb and flow across the French frontier and many of the most notable works of Vauban and Coehorn found themselves besieged by one side or the other, often by both sides in succession. The Flanders area had so often been the scene of battle in those days that every terrain feature of the country and every architectural feature of its works were well known to all the combatants, the possible combinations of tactical moves equally well known, and the business of conducting sieges became as formal, monotonous and pre-ordained as a game of draughts. And, as Fortescue pointed out, 'the French court was fond of sieges, because it could attend them in state and take charge of the operations with little discomfort or danger.'

Rarely was a siege taken to its ultimate conclusion; the besiegers, having made the 'practicable breach', rarely stormed the town, looting and laying waste. This was not in the rules; once the breach was made and a token skirmish had taken place, the town or fort surrendered gracefully and the pieces were re-arranged on the board ready for the next phase of the game. Generally speaking, when one considers that the opposing forces were fairly evenly matched, and that bastioned fortification was at the acme of its development, the resistance offered by the various works leads one to suspect that the manifold elaborations of trace were scarcely worth the effort expended in building them.

Thus, at Alt Brisach on the Rhine, which had the reputation of being the most strongly fortified place in Europe – built by Vauban in 1665–6 – the siege in 1702 – led by Vauban – resulted in capitulation in fourteen days, due, according to Vauban, to the fact that in the intervening years the course of the Rhine had altered and thrown up some islands which made nonsense of the original defensive plans. Ath, besieged once again in 1707, capitulated in fifteen days, Ghent in thirteen and Ostend in three. Bouchaine fell in fifteen days to the Allies in 1711 and, in turn, the French retook it in 1712 after a sixteen day siege. All in all, the wars of Marlborough and Eugène against Louis XIV were not calculated to display fortification at its best.

The Peninsular War did little to strengthen faith in

ATLANTIC OCEAN

Sta Cruz

Torres Vedras

1st LINE

Sobral

Arruda

2nd LINE

Mafra

Bucelas

Sintra

Queluz

LISBON

The Lines of Torres Vedras; in strict fact they were not lines in the continuous sense but a series of detached redoubts joined by natural obstacles.

fortresses. On the one hand the Spanish works occupied by the French were all elderly and in poor repair; and on the other hand the British Army under Wellington was singularly ill-provided with siege equipment, which is why the Peninsular sieges abound in valiant hand-to-hand exploits during assaults and escalades. But the worth of permanent fortification during the Peninsular War was entirely eclipsed by the remarkable performance of extempore fieldworks in the celebrated Lines of Torres Vedras. Here, north of Lisbon, Wellington's engineers aided by the Portuguese built a triple line of 114 redoubts connected by entrenchments and reinforced by ravines, dammed streams and such other obstacles as nature could be persuaded to provide, the whole forming a barrier across the Estremadura, between the River Tagus and the sea. The outer line was 29 miles in length, and Wellington's forces were distributed along it, averaging 1600 men per mile of work. There was little attempt at cleverness; little or no flank defence, no ravelins or hornworks, no mathematically derived trace. Yet Masséna, with over 100,000 men, forbore to attack it, knowing full well that it was too formidable an obstacle for him to overcome.

In 1832 Antwerp was besieged, one of the last times a great fortress was assailed by sap, parallel and smooth-bore guns in the classic manner. The investment began on 24th November, and after the practicable breach had been made on 23rd December the garrison surrendered before the assault could be made. It serves no purpose to go into the full details of the siege, but there was one feature which served as a pointer to the future: the use of howitzers and mortars by the French besieging army, on a scale greater than ever used before, reduced the interior of the works to a ruinous condition. A contemporary account stated that the victors, on entering the works, 'passed through a scene of desolation and ruin which baffles description. With the exception of the principal powder magazine, two or three service magazines and the hospital, not a building remained standing. The terrepleins of the bastions were ploughed into deep ruts by the shells; the gorges were encumbered with heaps of fallen rubbish; and though the casemates and subterranean communications were not perforated, all of them had sustained damage from the incessant explosion of shells and they emitted an almost insupportable odour, caused by the number of men who had crowded into them.

Just before the siege of Antwerp, the Prussians had begun to fortify Poznan (or Posen, as it was then), a task which occupied them until 1854, and cutting themselves loose from the theories of the previous century, they introduced the Polygonal or German System. The principal factor which led to the adoption of this system was the belated admission that artillery fire was not confined to flat trajectories and that the gunner did not necessarily have to see his target across the top of the gun barrel in order to hit it — the very fact of high-angle fire which was to be so strikingly underlined in the siege of Antwerp. The bastioned trace was designed to protect the escarp by cover from the flanks, but since the flanks themselves, as well as the escarp, could now be engaged at a distance by artillery there was little justification for the complication of the trace from that point of view. Moreover, from the defensive point of view the bastioned trace with its geometrical proportioning was weak in its direct artillery defence, since much of the rampart which ought to have been available for mounting guns, was in re-entering angles aligned for the defence of the flanks and curtains.

The polygonal trace had one supreme attraction; there was no longer any need to compute two-sevenths of the exterior side or set off angles of 100 deg. at the demi-gorge or perform any of the other myriad evolutions with pencil and compass demanded by the older systems. The work was built with faces as long as necessary and on such a trace as to make the best use of the available ground. The usual form of ditch with escarp and counterscarp surrounded the work, but was no longer necessarily parallel with the faces. In order to protect the faces and cover the ditch with flanking fire, the caponier was now developed in a fresh form, a masonry work reaching out into the ditch or even crossing it to connect with counterscarp galleries tunnelled beneath the glacis and the covered way. The caponier was loopholed for both musketry and case-shot-firing cannon; normally it was

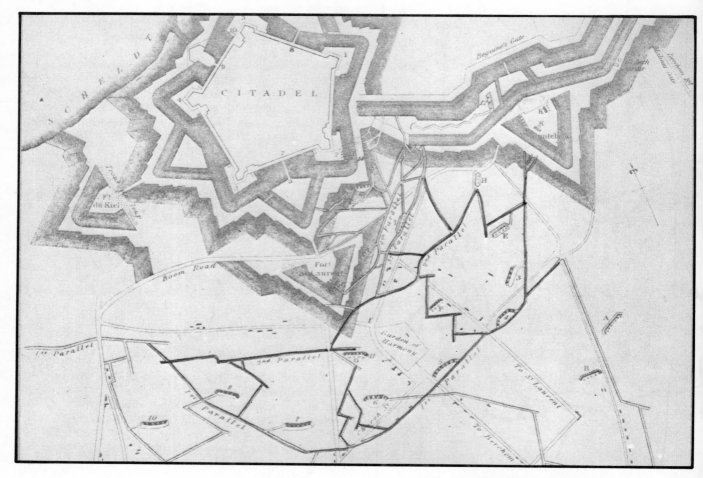

The Siege of Antwerp, 1832, one of the last formal sieges of the smoothbore era.

little more than a passageway with loopholes at each side, but, notably under German influence, it grew to two or even three stories in height in order to concentrate massive fire-power in the ditch. It also widened, to contain its own magazine, barrack rooms and even, in extreme cases, took on a rectangular form so as to include a parade ground.

The caponier leapt from virtual redundancy into premier place in the Prussian construction at Poznan, which was to be held up as the ultimate development of the Prussian system of fortification in the smoothbore artillery era. The forts were simple polygons, the faces running almost straight from angle to angle, merely bending slightly opposite the ditches of the ravelins (which were simple platforms for artillery) and the protection of the ditches and faces was assured by huge caponiers which staggered the beholders and caused a good deal of controversy. These caponiers crossed the ditch in the centre of each face and were two or three tiers high, their ends being protected by the ravelins. The inner ends passed through the rampart to flank its reverse slopes, the rampart being cut down to the depth of the main ditch and connected to the top of the caponier by drawbridges. The tops of the caponiers were covered with earth and provided with parapets;

and to carry things to their full conclusion, the corners of the caponiers actually had single-tier musketry caponiers to flank the faces of the caponiers themselves and to cover the re-entering ditch between the main structure and the rampart.

A covered way ran around the glacis of the ditch, but in place of simple traverses there were bomb-proof blockhouses or casemated barracks in the places of arms, all concealed beneath the crest of the glacis. The ravelins had their gorges closed by similar bomb-proof structures. Beneath the covered way a counterscarp gallery passed completely round the work, and tunnels ran forward beneath the glacis to extensive systems of countermine chambers. Another interesting feature was the adoption of a detached wall, an invention attributed to the Frenchman Carnot and commonly called a 'Carnot Wall'; the rampart was some distance back from the ditch, and the escarp wall rose above the edge of the ditch to form a free-standing wall, buttressed on the rear and provided with loopholes for musketry to fire across the ditch.

As said, the construction of the Poznan forts continued until 1854, a line of detached forts being built and then connected by a ditch and parapet. In 1875, however, it became obvious that the increased range and power of

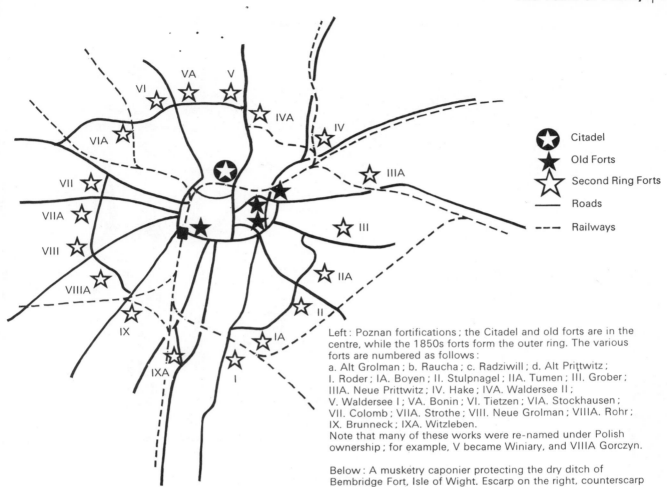

Left: Poznan fortifications; the Citadel and old forts are in the centre, while the 1850s forts form the outer ring. The various forts are numbered as follows:
a. Alt Grolman; b. Raucha; c. Radziwill; d. Alt Prittwitz;
I. Roder; IA. Boyen; II. Stulpnagel; IIA. Tumen; III. Grober;
IIIA. Neue Prittwitz; IV. Hake; IVA. Waldersee II;
V. Waldersee I; VA. Bonin; VI. Tietzen; VIA. Stockhausen;
VII. Colomb; VIIA. Strothe; VIII. Neue Grolman; VIIIA. Rohr;
IX. Brunneck; IXA. Witzleben.
Note that many of these works were re-named under Polish ownership; for example, V became Winiary, and VIIIA Gorczyn.

Below: A musketry caponier protecting the dry ditch of Bembridge Fort, Isle of Wight. Escarp on the right, counterscarp on the left. *George Z. Trebinski.*

rifled artillery, particularly with high-angle fire, had made the original ideas out of date. The masonry caponiers with their interior parades were now shell-traps, and the detached walls no more than ample targets, and the decision was taken to throw up a new ring of works around the old, a series of eleven detached forts some 3000 to 5000 yards forward of the earlier line and about 3–4000 yards apart, with six intermediate battery positions in the form of simple earthwork redoubts. A circular road was to join all this, and additional railway lines laid from the existing railways so as to form a connecting girdle within the line of works, with spur tracks running to the vicinity of the various forts and redoubts for purposes of supply.

As originally conceived this meant a 30-mile line, and the Governor of the fortress protested that while it might be a very pretty scheme on paper, the problems of manning it, supplying it and controlling it would be virtually impossible. In deference to this view, the plans were modified, bringing the line of works back closer to Poznan and thus shortening the perimeter to about 22 miles. Unfortunately, of course, this meant that the selected sites were second-best, which rather prejudiced their military worth, some of the forts being overlooked by high ground as little as 2000 metres away.

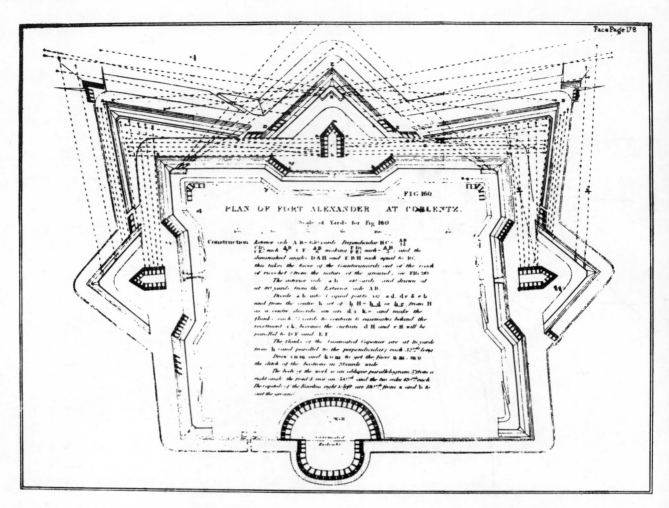

Face Page 178

FIG 160

PLAN OF FORT ALEXANDER AT COBLENTZ.

Scale of Yards for Fig 160

The design of these works was a vast change from the earlier forts; instead of commodious polygons, the trace was now, while still polygonal, such as to provide a wide front and minimum depth. Deep and narrow ditches surrounded each work, these being protected by low single-tier caponiers with ample overhead protection. The ramparts were of massive section, with bomb-proof casemates sunk into the rear faces giving ample accommodation for the garrison and stores.

The construction of this outer ring lasted until the turn of the century. In 1908 most of the older works were demolished, reliance henceforth being placed on the new outer line, but except for its use as a store depot and military headquarters during the First World War, the Fortress of Poznan never justified its existence. In 1939 the rapid advance of the German Army bypassed it and eventually some of the individual works were taken over by the Germans as store depots and military camps; perhaps the nadir of fortification was reached in the notorious Fort VII which became a Gestapo-run concentration and extermination camp. It is preserved today as a memorial to the martyrs of Poland who died there, but beyond that admirable purpose its preservation allows examination of a typical, relatively unaltered fort of the 1880s.

The Prussian polygonal system as used at Fort Alexander, Coblenz. Notice the completely detached caponiers and the interlocking fields of fire.

But by the latter part of the nineteenth century fortification had made some startling changes, and to understand why and what these changes were, it is necessary to go back a few years and look at coast fortification once more.

Coast defence, as a distinct branch of fortification engineering, received little recognition prior to the nineteenth century. This was not due to any failure to recognise the threat of a seaborne attack, but simply that such an attack would have differed very little in substance from the type of attack to be expected against a land work. A ship might be expected to bombard the shore, or a party of soldiers or marines might be landed in an invasion attempt: in either case the effect on the fort would be the same as if a land force were bombarding or besieging. As a result, when a work was placed in a position to guard the sea approach to a town or harbour it differed very little from the contemporary land works. Indeed, it would be fair to say that they *were* land fortifications, but they just happened to have one or two faces fronting the sea. The similarity was carried sufficiently far as to even provide wet ditches on the sea face, with

The main gate of Tilbury Fort, on the river Thames. *Ian Hogg.*

A gun emplacement on the ramparts of Tilbury Fort. *Ian Hogg.*

no more than a small retaining wall separating the two bodies of water. It is apparent that the engineers of those days were as much, if not more, concerned with securing the work against land attack as they were against attack from the sea.

This makes sense when one considered the difficulties of landing an army or even a raiding force from sailing ships by means of rowing boats ; such an exercise would be suicidal in the face of even a poor fort, and thus it would be a more sensible move for the attacker to land his forces at some undefended and remote beach and then march overland to launch an attack on the coastal town from the land side, possibly supporting it by ship bombardment in order to give the defenders two fronts to worry about.

It will be recalled that Henry VIII of England made a move toward specialised coast defence works, but this had never been copied, and indeed his castles had been allowed to deteriorate in the intervening years. In 1798 Thomas Blomefield, Inspector of Artillery, toured the various defences of England and reported on the state in which he found them.

'Deal Castle. There are fifty barrels of powder here, a considerable part of which is unserviceable. The window of the magazine is very dangerous and insecure. The guns have been long here . . .'

'Pendennis Castle. The upper floor . . . is cumbered with a quantity of camp equipage which was received from the Herefordshire Militia.'
'St Mawes. The guns are old excepting one 24-pounder. The carriages appear sound but want painting.'

Although the castles, doubtless due to Henry's constructors, were in better condition than some of the other defences :

'Hastings. Eleven 12-pounders mounted on the Sea Beach . . . the Guns carriages and shot being much exposed to the Spray of the Sea are exceeding damaged by it. The powder having been 20 years in store and one side of the Magazine being damp, six barrels have been rendered unserviceable and the remaining fourteen barrels are doubtful.
'Rye. In the Town of Rye are mounted six old 4 and 3-pounders Brass which were presented to the Corporation by Queen Elizabeth. Their carriages are quite decayed and the Guns seem very suspicious.'
'Carisbrooke Castle. Is used at present as a Hospital. The guns are all dismounted and their carriages broken up.'

Doubtless such depressing reading could have been duplicated elsewhere in the world as well. Due to the disenchantment with Henry's casemates, succeeding defences were always out in the open, usually on ramparts and firing through embrasures in the case of a major work, or behind a simple earth parapet for smaller batteries. Thus the equipment was exposed to the weather and the sea air, and since the personnel provided to look after the batteries usually consisted of a handful of pensioners and invalids, and since the upkeep of the equipment frequently devolved on the local inhabitants, it was hardly surprising that the defences were defective.

The Napoleonic Wars led to a general overhaul of the defences of the European coasts, but so far as Britain was concerned it was done in the knowledge that the

New York Harbour, 1852; Fort Tompkins on the left, and the casemates of Fort Richmond under construction in the foreground.

Royal Navy would be unlikely to allow a hostile fleet to come close enough to do any damage. On the other hand the French were at the receiving end of British Naval supremacy and had good reason to fear attacks from the English fleet. As a result the French coastal forts were brought to an efficient state and numbers of them which were considered insufficiently strong were re-built. It was during this reconstruction that Montalembert took a most decisive step, one which was to set the pattern for coast defences for a long time; he revived the casemate.

The drawbacks to the casemate were well enough known; confined space in which to work guns, blast, smoke and fumes, and a restricted field of fire. But on the other hand advances in weapons made the ramparts of a fort a distinctly unhealthy place on which to work guns. The ship of the line was now capable of firing shell, either powder-filled or, as developed during the Napoleonic Wars, shrapnel, both of which were far more lethal to a gun detachment on the ramparts than solid shot had been. Moreover it was becoming the fashion to station sharp-shooters in the tops of ships, and these frequently had command of a low-lying work and could pick off the gunners with relative ease. Finally the late eighteenth century saw the adoption of bomb-ships into many fleets, reinforced vessels in which mortars and howitzers were mounted; these could be used for ship-to-ship action, but their prime purpose was the shelling of the shore, and against these an open work was defenceless. On balance, the casemate now offered more advantages than drawbacks, and with reasonably intelligent design it was possible to provide the casemate occupants with sufficient room to move and work and sufficient fresh air to prevent their being immobilised by smoke and fumes.

Montalembert produced his first casemated work in the late 1780s and went on to build a number into existing forts on the Channel coast in the following 10 years. His lead was first followed by the Americans who, spurred on by the War of 1812, began a sizeable programme of coast defences on the North Atlantic coast and adopted the casemate form of construction. Fort Tompkins, New York, was probably the first to be completed, though it is a rather degenerate form of casemated construction, being little more than an updated version of one of Henry VIII's artillery castles. More in keeping with Montalembert's ideas, and indeed, exhibiting excellent design for its function, was Fort (or Castle) Williams on Governor's Island, New York Harbour.

The basic problem in coast defence gunnery in those days was bringing a sufficient weight of fire to bear on the target; loading the muzzle-loading smoothbore, running it out, firing, sponging, re-loading and running it back from where it had recoiled all took time. Fighting ranges were relatively short, and thus the guns had to be

The casemate of Montalembert, as he developed it for coast defence.

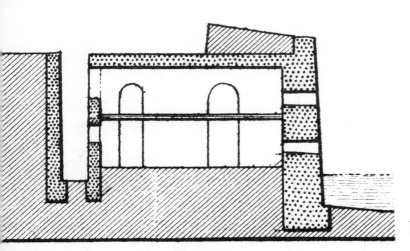

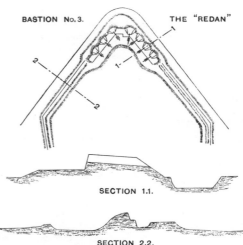

Sebastopol; the Redan at the beginning of the siege.

crammed together in order to get a reasonable number of shot into the target area in a short time. But no amount of cramming together on a rampart would ever equal the concentration afforded by a three-decker ship of the line. The casemate form of construction allowed vertical expansion by building the work as two or three tiers of casemates, and Castle Williams is one of the earliest (and best) examples of this trend. Basically a round (210 feet in diameter) tower, it had three tiers of casemates each mounting twenty-six guns on the seaward face, with space on the ramparts above for a further twenty-six guns, thus providing a concentration of fire which could outbid any contemporary warship.

The casemated battery of Castle Williams was 40 feet high, of sandstone, and with the wall 9 feet thick at the base, tapering to 7 feet at the roof level. The casemate ports were simple rectangular apertures about 4 feet square. Ventilation was assured, while the prospect of a ship's gun managing to put a roundshot or shell through a port was considered remote. Moreover the gun detachment, except during loading, would be well clear of the port and unlikely to be shot at by marksmen. The Americans continued to build casemated works based on this pattern for some years, though the impetus somewhat slackened when the problem of war receded. But little heed appears to have been paid to this activity by the European nations, and with the end of the Napoleonic era there was little activity in the coast defence field.

As it turned out, one of the catalysts in the revival of interest in coast defence was a land siege, one which reached epic proportions and, in the process, confounded many well-loved theories. Sebastopol, in the Crimean War, was a classic case of the right man in the right place being worth any amount of theory-derived masonry.

As a result of the Russo-Turkish War in 1828–9, in 1832 extensive plans were drawn up for the construction of permanent fortifications at Sebastopol, but all that

ever got built were a series of barracks which were intended to form defensible accommodation in the gorge walls of the main works; the rest of the works never even reaching the foundation stage. Early in 1854 hurried work began on preparing defences, and a number of open batteries protected by earthworks were first built. These were then extended by various barricades, detached loopholed walls and parapets, until eventually the area was completely ringed by earthworks. Due to the dilatory movements of the Allies, the defenders had until late September to complete these works, and by the time the British and French had landed and made their dispositions, the fortress mustered 172 guns to the attackers' 126.

The Siege of Sebastopol lasted 349 days; it was originally anticipated by the British that it would fall 'after a short cannonade' and the reasons which led to the prolonged defence are of considerable interest. Many excellent accounts of the siege exist, and this is no place to go over such well-trodden ground, but from the fortification aspect there are a number of points which, in the general accounts, escape notice. Moreover after the siege it was generally considered among military engineers that the situation at Sebastopol was the proverbial exception, and the schoolmen performed some remarkable gymnastics in attempting to show that the lessons of the siege actually bore out or reinforced classical teaching. One engineering text went so far as to say that 'the fact remains that the works . . . were never proof against assault' in spite of the fact that numerous assaults had failed dismally.

What helped to prolong the siege was the fact that Sebastopol was never completely isolated; the defenders had access to lines of supply, so that munitions, weapons

British mortar and gun batteries during the Siege of Sebastopol.

and men could be moved in to reinforce. As a result, when the siege ended the gun strength had risen to 982 guns of various calibres, and throughout the siege men were available to man and repair the defences. And instead of sitting inside their ramparts and waiting to be attacked, the defenders flew so far in the face of convention as to actually push their lines further out, constructing fresh redoubts and batteries.

Nevertheless, certain deficiencies in the works made themselves felt as the siege progressed, though it was not until Todleben, the engineer and commander of the defences, wrote an account in later years that the facts became generally known. The principal fault lay in the absence of bomb-proof accommodation; due to this, reserves had to be kept well back from the firing line in order to be safe from Allied howitzers and mortars, and thus, when they were needed, they took time to get into place. The maintenance and building of works absorbed a force varying between five and ten thousand strong and, inevitably, there were considerable casualties among the working parties: had bomb-proof shelter been readily available, they could have been rapidly withdrawn into them when bombardments began. Moreover the soldiers used on labouring tasks by day were in no condition to take their places in the defences at night, so that the effective armed strength of the defenders was often a good deal less than mere figures might suggest.

Two particular works remain historically attached to the siege of Sebastopol; the Redan and the Malakov Tower. The Redan was, at the commencement of the siege, no more than its name implies — a salient earthwork mounting seven guns, with a shallow dry ditch before it and earthen embrasures. At the flanks of the gun battery was a simple parapet and banquette, with an even shallower ditch. But by the close of the siege the working parties had laboured to such good effect that it blossomed into a complex of traversed gun platforms, reinforced parapets, extempore bomb-proofs and a deepened ditch, which repulsed British attacks with relative ease.

The Malakov Tower was a two-tiered casemated structure with rifle embrasures on top, and it was a considerable thorn in the side of the French. It was as much of a thorn in the Russian side, for it was an ill-designed work: it acted as a magnet for the Allied gunners who rapidly demolished the rifle gallery and the striking of shot drove splinters of masonry into the area, which proved highly dangerous to the occupants of the redoubt enclosing the tower. An additional hazard to these misfortunates was the occasional shot or shell which ricocheted or rebounded from the tower to land among the open batteries.

Eventually the French took the Malakov in an assault which astonished everybody by being over in about three minutes at comparatively small cost in casualties. It was hailed as a great feat of arms, and General Pelissier, the French Commander-in-Chief, was made Duke of

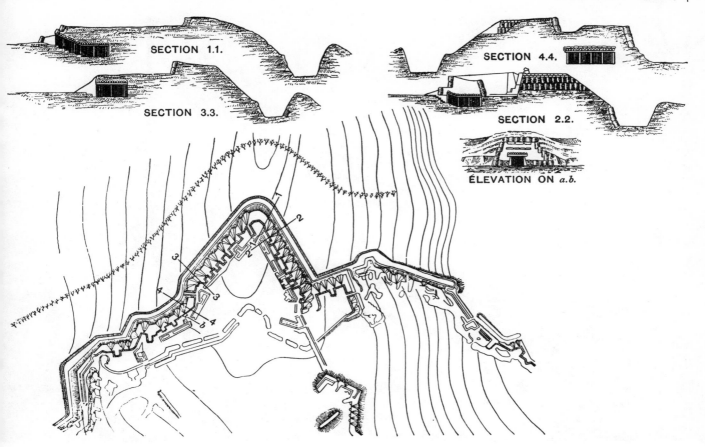

SECTION 1.1.

SECTION 3.3.

SECTION 4.4.

SECTION 2.2.

ÉLEVATION ON *a.b.*

Malakoff. Many years later an elderly survivor of the Crimean campaign revealed that the notable feat of arms was, in fact, as much a myth as any other French feat of arms. Pelissier had carefully watched the Malakov Redoubt for several days on end, and he eventually saw that the Russians were in the habit of marching out the defending force at the same hour each day, marching the fresh relief in a few minutes later. He therefore had his troops ready and, as he saw the defenders move out on their daily changeover, gave the order for the assault; the attack went in and the Malakov redoubt and tower were secured in the three minutes before the fresh relieving force could reach the position; and due to the disposal of the reserves previously mentioned, the French were able to consolidate their gain before a force could be assembled to evict them; of such things are legends made.

While Todleben's earthworks at Sebastopol were demonstrating their ability to absorb gunfire, further along the Russian coast another work was busy teaching lessons of another sort. On a strip of land separating the Dnieper river from the Black Sea, opposite Odessa, was the old fort of Kinburn. This had been built by the Turks at an uncertain date and passed into Russian hands, after one of their frequent disputes with the Turks, in 1774. It has proved impossible to obtain any plans of the work, but it seems to have been largely a bastioned rampart with guns en barbette, and firing through embrasures. Some eighty guns and twenty mortars were mounted

The Redan at the end of the siege, showing how it had been reinforced.

Sebastopol; the Malakov Tower.

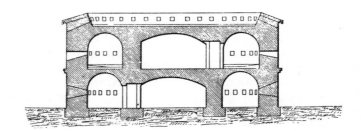

since, in company with Fort Ochakov across the river mouth, it was the principal guard to the entrance to the Dnieper.

On 17th October 1855 a combined British and French fleet appeared off Kinburn with the intention of reducing the fort and gaining entrance to the river. The fleet was largely composed of wooden steamships, but the French produced three 'armoured floating batteries' reputedly built to designs made by Napoleon III himself, but probably owing more to General Paixhans. These vessels bore 4-in. iron plating over 17 inches of wood on their sides, and they were each armed with sixteen 56-pounder Paixhans shell guns. While the remainder of the

fleet stood off out of harm's way, the *Devastation*, *Tonnante* and *Lave* steamed in to 800 yards range, anchored, and began systematically shelling the fort. They appeared to be presenting the Russian gunners with an ideal stationary target, and the defenders rapidly opened fire with 18- and 32-pounder guns firing solid shot, but the iron plating withstood the attack, being merely dented by the balls.

After four hours of duelling the French shells had thoroughly wrecked the interior of Kinburn, while the Russian fire, though obtaining some 200 hits on the three armoured ships, had only killed two and wounded twenty-five men, largely from chance shots and splinters entering the gun ports, and they had done nothing to reduce the intensity or accuracy of the French fire. The Russian commander surrendered; the fleet moved across and took up its positions off Fort Ochakov, and the commander of that work capitulated forthwith, without waiting to be bombarded.

The action at Kinburn was the birthplace of a number of theories and practices which had immeasurable effect in the years which followed. It confirmed the French in their belief that shell guns and iron armour were the next stage in the development of Naval architecture and armament, and this led them to lay down *La Gloire*, the first ironclad warship. This in turn led to ironclad construction in England, and from then on the development and improvement of armoured ships became a continuing process.

An incident in the Crimean War; the Allied fleet bombard Taganrog in May 1855. *National Army Museum.*

The other side of the coin was the appalling damage which the French guns had done to the land defences at Kinburn, which led directly to the conclusion that ships could at last pose a considerable threat to a coast battery, and that therefore the coast battery had to be extremely resistant to the ship's fire. The abortive expedition of the British fleet to Kronstadt in 1854, when the British bombardment had no effect except to demonstrate the difficulties inherent in using large ships in narrow and shallow waters, somewhat clouded the issue from the Navy's viewpoint, but the British Army rapidly came to the conclusion that their thoughts on coast battery design would have to be extensively revised in the light of the affair at Kinburn.

After the Crimean War, Napoleon III moved to assist the Italians and annexed Nice and Savoy as his price, which in British eyes at least confirmed their opinion that he was seeking to expand and might well decide to look across the Channel. The programme of ironclad-building in progress in France was also giving rise to alarm, and as a result of public clamour a Royal Commission sat in 1859 to consider the defences of Britain. In 1860 it reported, recommending the spending of over eleven million pounds on defensive forts and batteries, and by this action precipitated not only an immense building programme in Britain and the Empire but also in other countries which

La Gloire, the first ironclad of the French Navy. *John Freeman.*

hurried to follow suit. Germany, Belgium, Holland, Spain, Russia, America, Italy and Japan were soon vying with each other in the complexity and thickness of their coast defences, and the sums of money involved must have been astronomical.

The basic problem confronting the fort engineers was no longer protection against assault or siege, but protection against the ship's gun; and the ship's gun had suddenly become a much greater threat, because it was now protected by armour. Therefore the ship's gun had to be capable of penetrating the armour on the expected enemy vessel; therefore it was likely to have a penetrating power which boded ill for a fort. Furthermore, since the ship was armoured, it could, as it had done at Kinburn, move close in and anchor so as to employ its guns to best effect; therefore the fort had to have even more powerful and longer-ranging guns in order to discourage this manoeuvre. And so it went on; what it all boiled down to was that the fort had to be equally well armoured and better armed than the ship, or vice-versa, depending on whether your point of view was naval or military.

It was in this climate of opinion that the casemate was embraced with fervour, particularly since an American engineer, Joseph W. Totten, had been experimenting for some years in attempts to reduce the size of the casemate port in order to reduce the danger to the occupants. He eventually produced his 'Armoured Throat' casemate in which an iron plate was let into the masonry so as to

leave an aperture large enough to allow the gun muzzle to be poked through but small enough to reduce the chances of enemy missiles finding their way in. He later improved his design by developing hinged shields which could be closed except when the gun was actually ready to fire, but this refinement appears not have caught on in Europe; there was always the fear that a chance shot might derange the hinges or otherwise jam the shutter closed, putting the gun out of action. But apart from that, Totten's use of armour was seized upon, and a wide variety of armour plate techniques tried out.

In Britain a prolonged series of trials of various systems of iron armour in casemates ensued, one unlooked-for result of which was that it held up the construction of the forts called for by the Royal Commission until this very basic matter had been resolved. Eventually a system of construction using multiple plates separated by 'elastic filling' — usually wood or asphalt — was agreed upon, and casemated iron armoured works were built accordingly. One of the best existing examples of the style evolved is to be seen at Bovisand Fort in Plymouth Sound.

The gun battery of 9-in. and 10-in. rifled muzzle-loading guns was in a curved-front casemate structure of granite, 9 feet thick. The gun ports formed in this masonry face were filled with plate armour composed of three 5-in. plates separated by 5-in. layers of iron asphalt.

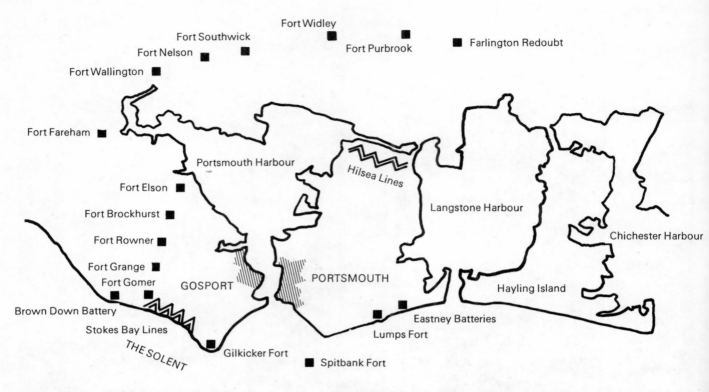

Above: Portsmouth and its 19th century defences

A 68 pounder RML gun on carriage and slide at Southsea Castle. *Mike Jarvis*

Top Left : An open caponier in the rampart musketry gallery of Fort Widley. The parts at the sides command the gallery while those at the end cover the roof of the ditch caponier *Mike Jarvis*

Above : The gorge wall and caponier of Fort Widley *Mike Jarvis*

Below : Fort Widley rampart, ditch and glacis. The musketry gallery and its caponier are in the foreground, the ditch caponier beyond. *Mike Jarvis*

A 9 inch 12 ton Rifled Muzzle Loading gun, typical of the armament of coast defences 1870-1890 *Mike Jarvis*

Fort Widley, west caponier and mortar battery.
Mike Jarvis.

Far Left: Rampart emplacements at Fort Widley *Mike Jarvis*

Left: Fort Widley, the ditch, with a two-tier flanking caponier with musketry and cannon ports covering the main ditch, and a single-tier musketry caponier covering the salient of the ditch. *Mike Jarvis.*

— a material made up of a mixture of cast iron swarf, asphalt, bitumen and pitch — and supported on a framework of 2-feet-square iron bars. The casemate chambers were vaulted stone and brickwork surmounted by a roof of $2\frac{1}{2}$ feet of brickwork topped with $2\frac{1}{2}$ feet of concrete and surfaced with asphalt. The remainder of the work was little more than a curtain wall, protection against land attack being achieved by a substantial flanking ditch with a caponier covering it.

The rear of the casemate gallery opened on to an arched verandah, and the casemates were closed by wood and glass screen walls. These, together with partitions between the casemates, rendered them sufficiently warm and dry for the detachments, for the casemates were their living quarters as well as their fighting compartments. These flimsy partitions were to be removed when action threatened, since trial firings had shown that this form of construction could scarcely survive the blast of a 10-in. gun fired inside the casemate, and the timber and glass were liable to be blown about with lethal effect.

This type of casemated work was considered satisfactory for the majority of positions; usually at water level and at such distance from the deep water channel as to prevent an enemy vessel from getting too close. But there were some localities where a considerable body of water had to be denied to an enemy, too great a breadth to be covered from the adjacent shore due to the limited range of the guns then in use. A notable instance was Spithead Roads between Portsmouth and the Isle of Wight; here there was a wide area of water in which a fleet could manoeuvre or even anchor to bombard the naval dockyard, without being endangered by the fire of batteries on the mainland or on the island. The only solution was to construct forts on convenient shoals in the middle of the water, and plans were drawn up for the construction of three-tier masonry casemated works with additional guns and mortars on the roof, for,

Above: An old type of casemate, without armour, in Point Battery, Portsmouth. The traversing pivot and racer can be seen in the floor, and the hooks in the wall are for the gun rammer and sponge. *Mike Jarvis.*

Below: A similar casemate, from an old print, fully occupied. Right: A massive two-tier musketry caponier flanking the entrance to Scraesdon Fort, Plymouth. *Ian Hogg.*

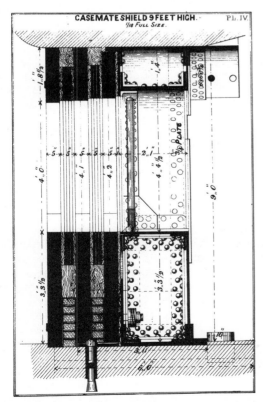

A casemate shield for a single-tier fort, using three layers of five-inch wrought iron separated by five-inch layers of wood and concrete, the whole supported by a framing of three-quarter-inch iron girders.

as the Royal Commission had pointed out, 'The adoption of such a mode of construction will add considerably to the amount of fire which can be brought to bear on any point and will give the upper tier of guns command over the decks of the attacking ships . . . .

But when the various trials of armour and casemate construction had been carried out, the plan was modified. The principal hazard here was that since the forts were out in the sea, ships could approach quite close, and there was thus the danger of the forts being exposed to heavy gun fire at short range. The casemate trials had shown that the iron armour plating would still remain fit to protect whatever was behind it even after the masonry portion of the fort had been demolished by continuous firing at short range, and because of this it was decided that the sea forts would not use masonry but would instead be entirely faced with armour. This had, in fact, been tried by the Russians at Kronstadt some years previously, by hanging iron plates outside the masonry to give additional protection, but the British design used masonry only for the foundation and central section of the work, the outer face and casemate floors being solely of iron plate fastened to an iron framework.

Four of these iron forts were eventually built: one at the end of the breakwater in Portland Harbour; one behind the breakwater in Plymouth Sound; and two, known as Horse Sand and No Man's Land Forts, from the shoals on which they stood, in Spithead Roads. In addition there were three more of compound construction, having armoured faces to the sea and masonry faces to the land side: Fort Cunningham, Bermuda; St Helen's Fort off the

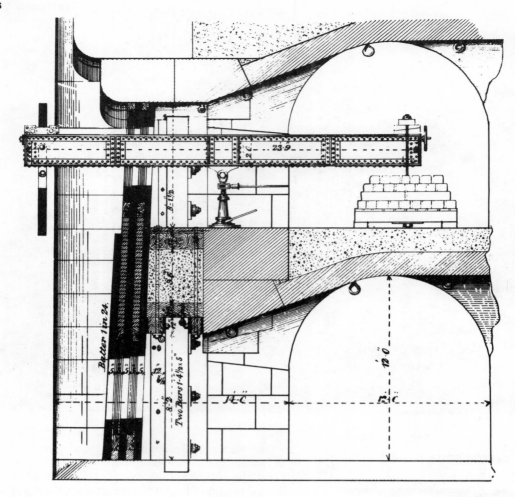

The armoured face of Garrison Point Fort, Sheerness; the two tiers of masonry casemates are closed by triple shields of wrought iron armour. The final plate is shown here in the process of being brought into place by a traveller.

Isle of Wight; and Spitbank Fort in Spithead, close to the Portsmouth shore. The compound construction, which of course economised in armour, was considered sufficient in these cases, since warships could not approach the masonry faces due to shallow water and the proximity of the shore.

The exact dimensions varied, of course, with each fort, but, as an example, Horse Sand Fort began with the building of a 231-feet diameter ring of masonry 53 feet 6 inches thick and sunk into the sand. This ring was faced with granite and filled with Portland Stone to a level of 11 feet below the low water line. On top of the stone. the ring was filled with clay and shingle until level with the top of the masonry, where a solid concrete cap was laid. On this solid base an outer wall 16 feet high and 14 feet 6 inches thick, of granite and Portland Stone, was built, 100 feet in diameter, reaching to a height 16 feet above the high water mark. At this point a ring of wrought iron 3 inches thick and 3 feet wide was set into the masonry to form the base for the iron structure.

In the centre of the work a masonry tower was raised which acted as a core, supporting portions of the iron structure and carrying ammunition lifts, offices, stores and other domestic necessaries, the magazines being built within the stone ring, below the water level. Vertical steel casings 12 feet deep, 7½ feet high and triangular in form were bolted to the iron base ring to form buttresses between the casemates, and on top of these rested another solid ring of 3-in. iron forming a continuous support for the second tier of the work. More triangular casings were bolted to this, and on it were laid radial girders, their inner ends supported by the masonry centre tower. Finally a third iron ring went on top of the second tier buttresses, and more girders were laid in to the centre. Arch plates were bolted between the radial girders to form a floor for the second tier and a roof, and finally 4½ feet of concrete was laid on top of the roof girders and plates to give bomb-proof protection.

The face of the work was now armoured by firstly fitting vertical support bars between the upper and lower iron rings and then bolting the armour plate to them. Firstly came a 5-in. plate, laid horizontally, one plate sufficing for each tier; then a 1-in. layer of cement and wood, and then the middle plate layer. These plates, 22 feet 6 inches high, were applied vertically to span both tiers, and varied in thickness; if the plate covered a casemate and contained a gun port, it was 7 inches thick;

Armoured casemates of Bovisand Fort, Plymouth, showing the granite face and armoured shields. *Ian Hogg.*

Left: The interior of a casemate at Bovisand Fort. The curved bar across the shield top is to carry a mantlet of woven rope, intended to act as a curtain to keep small-arms fire and shell splinters out of the casemate. *Ian Hogg.*

Spitbank Fort; the armoured face, which originally carried nine 12.5-in. rifled muzzle-loading guns in the casemates. The fort is 151 feet in diameter at water level and cost just under £200,000 to build. *Portsmouth City Museum.*

Map of the defences of Portsmouth, showing the location of the iron forts.

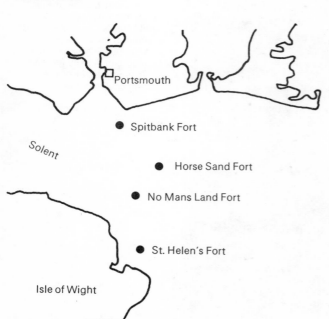

if it covered a buttress it was 5 inches thick. After another layer of 6 inches of iron concrete, a final layer of 5-in. plate, laid horizontally as the first, was applied.

The total amount of armour was 3764 tons, and although the precise cost of the fort is impossible to determine, due to the involved accounting systems in use, it is estimated at about £437,000 complete with its planned armament of twenty-five 10-in. and twenty-four 12.5-in. muzzle-loading guns. While the all-armoured fort was a technical *tour de force*, it was an expensive exercise, and it was only warrantable where there was no alternative system of covering the water gap.

But even while these works were being built, advances in ordnance and ammunition were making them obsolescent. On the continent the great ironmasters of the Ruhr were convinced that wrought iron was merely a step in the right direction, and they were hard at work trying with one hand to produce better protective materials and with the other, as it were, trying to develop even more efficient methods of attacking armour. At the same time, governments intent on building coast defences canvassed for the best weapons and the best protection, holding contests open to all comers to see who could produce either armour plate to defeat attack by a specified combination of gun and shot or a gun and shot that was capable of piercing some standard target. The records of the 1870s and 1880s abound with these 'competitions': the Schveningen Competition in 1879 when the Dutch tried a variety of piercing

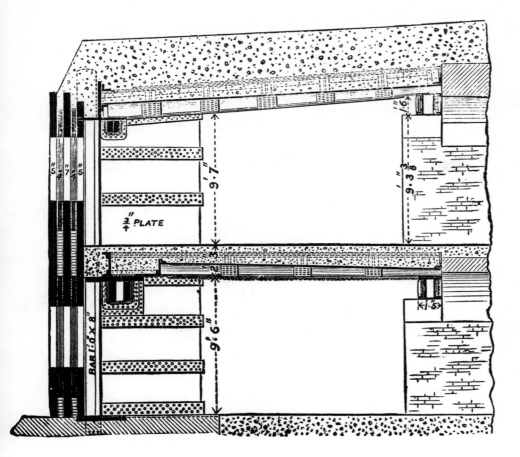

Section of No Man's Land fort in Spithead Roads. The masonry core supports the iron framework which is protected on the outer face by 19 in. of armour in three plates. The upper framework is covered by four and a half feet of concrete. The work cost about £465,000 and was armed with 24 10-in. and 24 12.5-in. rifled muzzle-loading guns.

projectiles against standard plates; the Spezia Trial of the same year of the Armstrong 100-ton 17.72-in. muzzle-loading gun firing a variety of competing shells; more trials at Spezia in 1882 against 48-cm. iron plates, and the Bucharest Cupola Competition in 1885–6 when the Roumanian government sought to discover a perfect system for the protection of forts. All these, and many more, produced a wealth of data, most of which was violently contradictory and much of which was of value only until the results of the next trial were announced.

The heart of the matter was the constant leap-frogging between the development of armour protection and the development of a projectile capable of defeating it – a process which continues to the present day. Wrought iron armour came into being simply because it was the only hard substance available that was capable of being fabricated in large enough pieces. It was proof against the normal round shot and early pointed wrought iron shot from rifled guns, and in order to defeat it the Palliser shot was evolved. This was a cast iron projectile, with the nose section chilled during the casting process so as to develop an extremely hard point. To counter this, armour of the same type, cast iron with the face chilled so as to harden it, was developed by Gruson of Germany. Instead of merely producing flat slabs for incorporation into masonry structures, Gruson invented a system of making cast curved sections which contained gun ports and which could be fitted together to produce a continuous casemate of any desired length, the face of which

curved back to meet a masonry and concrete roof. This had the considerable advantage that a pointed shot was likely to ricochet from the curved surface and glance over the top of the work instead of, as with a vertical plate, penetrating.

Gruson armour was first tried in Prussia in 1868, then by Russia in 1871 and 1873. The result of firing a 28-ton Krupp gun at a specimen shield, at a range of only 10 yards, was astonishing; the 517-lb shot disintegrated as it struck, leaving no more than a rough spot a few millimetres deep on the face of the armour. As a result, Prussia adopted the Gruson system for new batteries to be built on the lower River Weser, while Belgium built a number on the Scheldt to protect the approaches to Antwerp. Austria and Italy also adopted Gruson's shields for use in land forts, but before much more could be done Gruson developed a much better idea which soon relegated casemate shields to secondary importance; this was the 'Gruson Cupola'.

The idea of a revolving armoured turret to protect guns had begun as a Naval proposal with the simple structure of Captain Cowper Coles RN. This began as a simple shield mounted on a turntable, and then became a covered circular box with a gun or guns inside, firing through ports. The idea was taken up by various nations and by the early 1870s the turret had become an accepted feature of ironclad warships. Not unnaturally, its possibilities as a land defence measure were not long in being brought to notice; as early as 1863 a Lieutenant

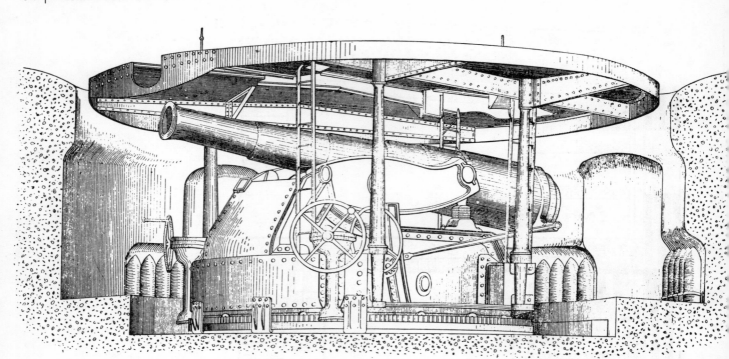

Above: A disappearing coast gun concealed within a concreted pit and covered with an iron shield. The gun is down, for loading.

Below: The disappearing gun 'up' for firing. This mode of mounting rapidly supplanted the casemate since it did not present the ship with a permanent target.

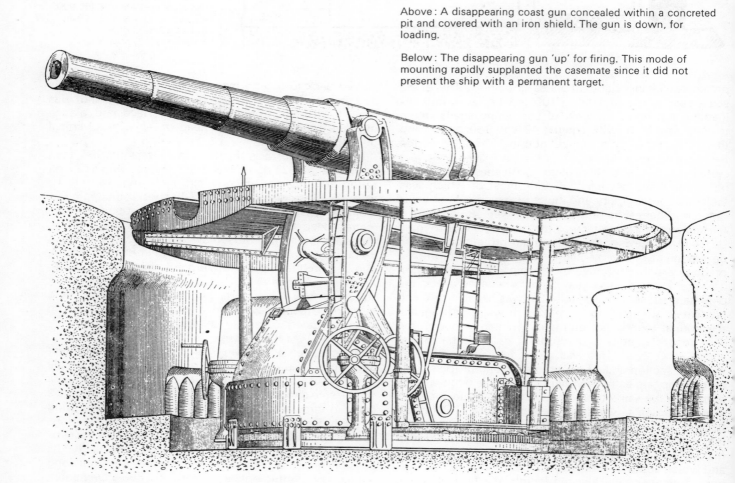

Left: Erecting a Gruson armoured casemate battery on the banks of the River Weser in Germany.

Below: One of the cast-iron sections making up a Gruson cupola.

Duncan of the Royal Artillery published a paper 'On the Adaptation of the Cupola of Captain Coles to Modern Fortresses', one of his many suggestions being to fit cupolas to the tops of Martello Towers. But there was a considerable body of opinion holding the belief that an armoured turret was too delicate; a chance shot might easily jam its movement or derange its pivot. In seaborne applications the chances of such a shot were considered negligible, but in land defences — static targets arrayed against static guns — the risk was too great.

Numerous experiments soon showed that the risk had been grossly overestimated. Probably the most convincing display was the trial in Portland Harbour in 1872, when HMS *Hotspur* was anchored 200 yards from HMS *Glatton* and fired two shots from a 12-in. gun at the *Glatton*'s turret. Both struck the turret with a force estimated at just under 7000 foot-tons, and penetrated the turret plating to a depth of about 15 inches; a kid, a rabbit and a hen, which had been placed inside the turret,

showed no ill-effects, and the turret still revolved freely.

After this, the turret was regarded more kindly, and within a short time a scheme was evolved to erect a two-gun turret mounting 16-in. rifled muzzle-loading guns on the end of the Admiralty Pier at Dover. The defences there were some distance from the shore, due to the terrain, and due to the layout of the harbour an iron fort was not considered feasible. The only way to get heavy defences well forward and well protected was the turret, and it was due to these unusual circumstances that the installation at Dover was the only turret battery ever completed in the British defences. It should be noted, however, that there was considerable enthusiasm for a policy of installing turrets on top of several forts in order to augment their gun power. The armoured sea forts at Spithead had their roofs reinforced during construction for the subsequent addition of turrets, and other casemated masonry works were earmarked for roof-mounted turrets. None of these proposals ever came about, for two

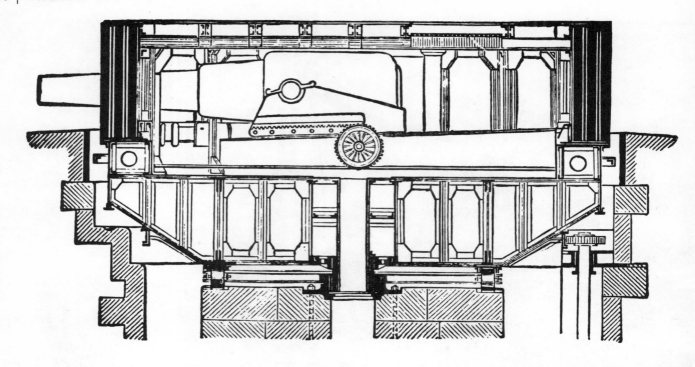

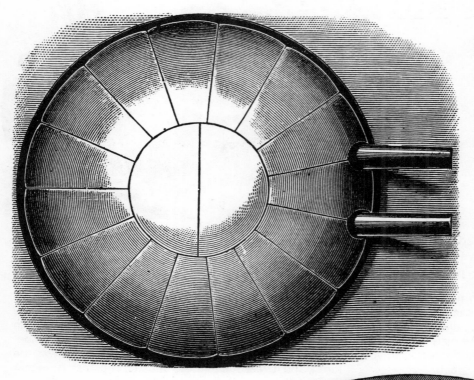

Above: Section of the 16-in. gun turret at Dover, showing how the superstructure revolved around a masonry pedestal by a roller race.

Left and below: The Gruson turret designed for two 17.72-in. guns at Spezia. Note the iron armoured glacis surrounding the turret at ground level in order to deflect shot which might otherwise jam the mechanism of rotation.

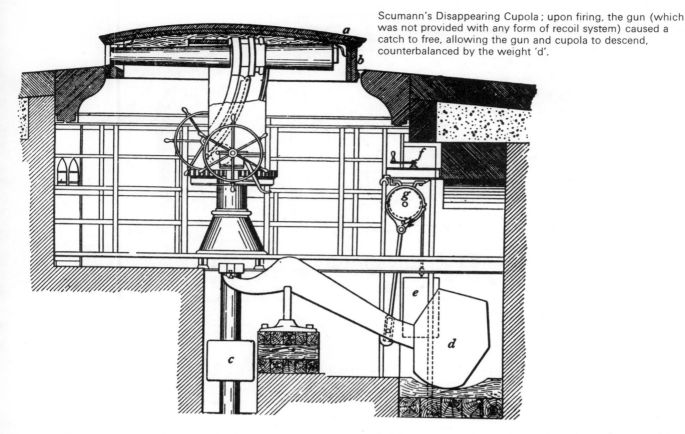

Scumann's Disappearing Cupola; upon firing, the gun (which was not provided with any form of recoil system) caused a catch to free, allowing the gun and cupola to descend, counterbalanced by the weight 'd'.

reasons; firstly the vast expense of an armoured turret, and secondly the equally vast weight, which had been sadly underestimated. When the Dover turret was finally completed in 1886 the all-up weight of the installation was 895 tons. The addition of five turrets (as was proposed for Horse Sand Fort, for example) would had added another 4500 tons or so to the load on the frame of the work and might very well have brought about its collapse.

The Dover turret was a relatively simple structure of vertical sidewalls and flat roof, multiple plated with wrought iron. Gruson now took the basic idea of a turret and allied it to his curved-face casting technique to develop an extremely efficient design which became the model for almost all subsequent land fortification applications. By using suitably cast segments, a turret could be put together relatively easily, and further cast units were produced to be built around the lower edge of the revolving structure to act as a glacis and thus preventing projectiles or splinters from lodging and preventing rotation. The joints between the segments were sealed by running in a molten mixture of lead and zinc.

The first of Gruson's cupolas to be employed in a work appear to have been a number supplied to the German government for installation near Bremerhaven. Contemporary drawings suggest that they were simply set down on a concrete foundation, the traversing ring concealed behind brickwork and a cast iron glacis plate, and then the lower section masked by an earthen parapet some distance in front. But this design was soon super-

seded by a system in which the body of the turret was carried in an underground concrete and masonry structure and only the armoured top was visible above the ground. The lower edge was protected by a glacis plate set in concrete, so that everything that could be seen was virtually impervious, both from the hardness of the armour and the compound curvature of the plate. This form was adopted for the turret to house the enormous 16-in. guns protecting the Italian naval base at Spezia, as well as by the German designers of coast defences on the Baltic shore.

But more attention was paid to Gruson's turrets by the designers of land defences than ever was by coast engineers. The millennium had arrived: here was an absolutely foolproof and invulnerable system of defence, and it was seized upon enthusiastically by engineers and by a number of gentlemen whose enthusiasm outran their ability. Turrets — or cupolas — were 'The Thing', and many and varied were the designs proposed; almost as many as the designs of forts in which to install them.

Foremost among the designers was Lieut-Colonel Schumann, originally of the Prussian Army Engineers, later the principal turret designer for Gruson. From the basic and simple armoured mushroom, Schumann's designs blossomed into a number of mechanical complexities intended to improve the degree of protection and the firing ability of the protected weapon. One design was for a retractable cupola, counterbalanced by a large weight on the end of a lever; the gun and turret were normally concealed, the roof of

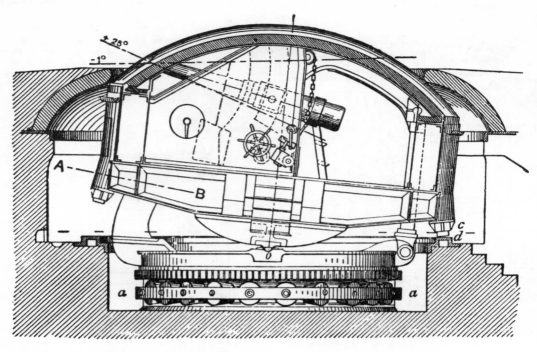

Mougin oscillating cupola for two 150-mm. guns.

Below: M. Mougin's plan for a subterranean fort protected by cupolas.

the turret being at ground level. By use of a hand gear the whole assembly could be raised to allow the gun clearance to fire, and the recoil automatically released a trip mechanism so that the turret sank down once again as soon as the gun had fired.

Another Schumann design was for an armoured cupola buried in the ground except for its upper surface into which was built a peculiar short-barrelled 21-cm. howitzer with its barrel shaped into a sphere; this rested on a recess in the turret, acted as a mantlet to keep the aperture closed, and also acted as a bearing surface for swinging the weapon in any direction. No recoil absorbing mechanism was provided, since the force generated by firing the mortar was transferred directly to the turret and through this to the ground.

In France, a M. Mougin, designer for the St Chamond gunmaking company, weighed in with a number of cupola designs which far exceeded those of Schumann in their complexity. Illustrated is an 'oscillating cupola' for two 15-cm. guns, which could be tipped forward to conceal the guns and back to expose their muzzles for firing. Mougin then took his ideas a stage further by developing a specimen fort to which his cupolas might be allied. This was to be a monolithic concrete mass, largely underground. Only the upper surface, which was to be provided with retractable cupolas, was visible. There was to be no ditch, no outworks, no parapets or ramparts; local protection was to be entirely dependent upon fire-power, the gun cupolas being augmented by smaller ones mounting machine guns, and between them these were held capable of beating off any attack.

Mougin proposed that a number of such forts should be disposed around the town or other protected place, connected by a line of rampart, behind which a railway line was to run. On this line were to be a variety of guns mounted on disappearing carriages on top of railway wagons; these carriages would allow the gun to fire over the top of the rampart without exposing the gunners to view, and their recoil would bring them below the rampart for re-loading.

Finally came General Brialmont, who also embraced the cupola with fervour, proposing to employ fixed and retractable models, though using a more-or-less conventional bastioned or polygonal fort as his basis. To understand the reason for this sudden enthusiasm for land defence, we must go back a little and see what had happened in Europe while the coast defence engineers had been at work.

The construction at Poznan, previously mentioned, was well under way before the perfection of Gruson's cupolas; moreover the German Army were of the opinion that such refinement would be unnecessary on that front. But there were several other nations who were less sanguine about their potential enemies and who began, about the 1880s, to plan new defences incorporating all the refinements which the ironmasters and mechanical engineers could offer, together with the stark simplicity of the polygonal trace. Nations as apparently unthreatened as Hungary and Roumania began erecting huge fortresses at colossal expense. And the greatest endeavours were by Belgium and France, both of whom had been made extremely wary by the events of 1870, when the Prussian Army streamed across the French border and appeared to be little deterred by the elderly fortresses which they met.

France, during the years of Napoleon Bonaparte, did little work on her land defences, largely, one might assume, because Napoleon's strategy did not envisage fighting on or about French soil. The major fortresses remained as Vauban had left them. But after Antwerp, the French seem to have had second thoughts; their success there demonstrated that against newer artillery techniques the ravelin and hornwork seemed of little utility. Then in 1830 and 1832 there were Republican uprisings, with barricades up in the Paris streets, and sundry other manifestations of a Revolutionary character. With the task of bolstering the precarious position of Louis Philippe, the Army decided to look to its fortifications, and, in particular, those of Paris. At that time Paris was largely dependent on its wall, but this was now augmented by a double ring of forts; in 1815 Blücher had appeared on the heights of Issy-le-Moulineaux to the South, and the memory of this seems to have been the deciding factor in determining the siting of the first line, some two kilometres outside the city wall. This was then to be augmented by a thin outer line about 5 kilometres in advance.

The Paris forts were not well conceived; the designers appear to have been caught between the Scylla of Vauban-type complexity and the Charybdis of the plain polygonal trace. The result was a unfortunate bastard form of quadrilateral traces with bastions at the angles. The first conception, indeed, had been to surround Paris completely with a second, bastioned, wall, an enormous structure wandering over hill and dale ignoring topography and the elementary principles of tactics alike' as one critic put it. But since this was obviously ridiculous, and incredibly expensive, it was rapidly abandoned for the ring of forts.

A feature of these works remarked upon by observers in later years was that they were so built as to be capable of all-round defence; there was no 'face to the country' on one side with a relatively weak gorge on the other; and the question raised itself of the pessimism of the constructors, who were obviously, or so it seemed, resigned to a strong force penetrating between the works to take them in reverse. In reality this was not quite the whole story; the forts were built as much to control Paris as to defend it. With the memory of the recent risings, and earlier anti-authoritarian antics of the Parisians, there was no telling what direction the forts might need to fire in when the time came, so in order not to be caught out they were designed to be capable of handling trouble from any direction. Indeed, one record asserts that the city wall was strengthened at this time in order that 'it might not appear to the People that Paris was to be bombarded during a riot'.

Fort Issy can be taken as an example of these works; the trace was a regular pentagon with sides of about 300 metres. The angles are formed into bastions and the

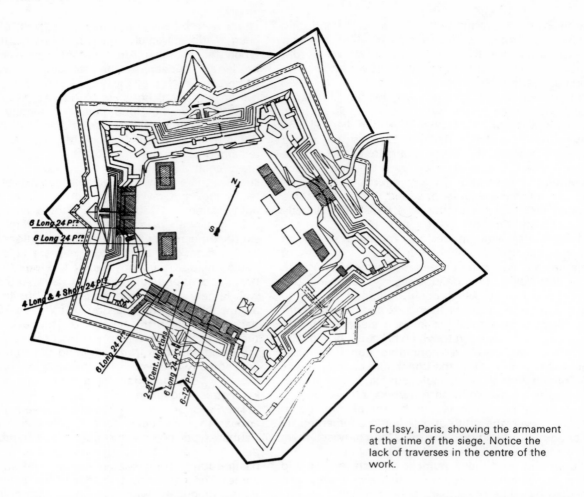

6 Long 24 Pr.s
6 Long 24 Pr.s
4 Long & 4 Short 24 Pr.s
6 Long 24 Pr.s
2-21 Cent. Mortars
6 Long 24 Pr. Pcs.
6-12 Pr.s

Fort Issy, Paris, showing the armament at the time of the siege. Notice the lack of traverses in the centre of the work.

work surrounded by a ditch. On the outer side of this ditch was the usual counterscarp wall, surmounted by a wide covered way which was separated from the crest of the glacis by a palisade fence. Opposite the centre of each face was a tenaille to cover the ditch, and on the outer side the glacis was formed into a species of ravelin resembling an overgrown place of arms. The escarp walls resembled those under erection at this time in Poznan, being extended above the earthwork to form a sort of Carnot Wall in front of the rampart, although this feature was not constructed in all the Paris forts nor, indeed, was it continuous in those works where it did appear.

Internally, much of the place was empty, bomb-proof accommodation being provided beneath portions of the rampart; but there was no form of traversing and due to the clear area in the centre a battery on any one face could take the opposite faces in reverse by ricochet fire with the greatest of ease, probably doing more good thereby than it would have done battering at the escarp wall.

With Paris secure, it was the turn of the Northern frontier; but work there was slow in starting and slower still in proceeding. The rise of Prussia, however, combined with the militarism of Napoleon III — who is reputed to have said that the stability of his rule depended on having

a war every 4 years — led to increased efforts around Metz and Belfort, which were stimulated to even greater speed by the events in Denmark in 1864.

In that year the Danish fortress of Duppel was besieged by the Prussian Army in the traditional sap and parallel manner. The defensive line consisted of a number of redoubts about 200 yards apart; these were simple earthwork parapets with artillery firing through embrasures, an infantry breastwork and a ditch. Within, each had a bomb-proof blockhouse in the gorge, which, being considerably higher than the crest of the parapet, was clearly visible and served to locate works which might otherwise have been easily concealed. When considered against the powerful masonry works being built in France, these were mere field fortifications, liable to fall to a corporal's guard. But in fact the Prussians spent from February 12th to April 18th investing Duppel, and finally carried it more by luck than good management.

The Prussians had arrayed 122 guns against Duppel, and placed the several redoubts under heavy bombardment; as a result, and due to the lack of bomb-proof shelter inside the redoubts, it was impossible to retain troops on the ramparts permanently. The Danish commander was in the habit of keeping the garrison in position at night, ready to repel attack, and then, fearing bombardment, withdrawing them to the gorge bomb-proof during the day. Consequently when the Prussians bombarded early one morning, and followed this up with an assault at the unheard-of hour of 10 a.m., the works were practically empty, and before the garrisons could get out of their bomb-proofs and inside the redoubts, the Prussians had taken the positions.

The ability of Duppel's simple earthworks to soak up punishment was singularly ignored ; most of the comment in other armies seems to have been to the effect that had it been properly laid out, with casemates, caponiers, ravelins and other artifices, it would have held out even longer. And yet at this same time reinforcement of the advantages of simple works was coming from across the Atlantic.

In the course of the American Civil War a number of forts, particularly coast defence works, became focal points for attack, and in many cases the attackers possessed rifled artillery. The results were quite surprising. Permanent works suffered, while temporary works took bombardment and absorbed it in a startling manner. Fort Pulaski was a pentagonal work of brick, a single casemate tier surmounted by barbette guns on the roof ; in April 1862 it was besieged by Federal troops with thirty-six guns, ten of which were rifled. At a range of 1700 yards these rifled guns breached an angle of the fort relatively easily, while the smoothbores severely damaged the rest of the work.

Fort Wagner, on the other hand, was an extempore work largely consisting of sand ramparts and with ample bomb-proof cover for the garrison. By sheltering in the bomb-proofs during the artillery bombardments and then manning the parapets, the defenders were able to beat off attack after attack with small arms fire with comparative ease. Forty-five guns were eventually deployed against the work, and although some 1173 shells landed on the bomb-proof, it was still habitable, while the uncounted shells which struck the sand parapets made little impression. The fort eventually surrendered after holding out for fifty-eight days.

These and similar events led to a certain amount of discussion on the relative virtues of masonry and earth as protective materials. It certainly led the American engineers to turn their faces against large casemated works and more to the development of open batteries for coast defence. But in Europe little heed seems to have been paid to the implications of Pulaski's and Wagner's relative resistive power. The French began improving their northern frontier forts on much the same lines as they had built the Paris ones. But before his engineers could finish the task, Napoleon III precipitated the Franco-Prussian War of 1870.

The common impression of the War of 1870 is that the Prussians stampeded all over the French and the expensive fortifications were of no avail, but this is a considerable over-simplification. In fact eighteen of the twenty-four forts in the path of the invasion sustained sieges of durations varying from one day to sixty-seven days, and there can be no doubt that without the forts to delay them the advance of the Prussians would have

been even faster. The principal reason for the fall of the various works can be largely lumped together under the general heading 'Lack of Preparedness'. It is of little worth to erect a massive defensive work and then man it, in the face of a determined and skilful enemy, with a scratch force of local volunteers with outdated armament and inadequate supplies, which was the case in many of the frontier forts. Moreover the command of a fortress under siege calls for a strong and forceful personality of considerable military ability, and this, with one or two notable exceptions, was what was missing, not only from the fortresses but from the rest of the French Army too.

Another significant feature was the ability of the Prussian artillery to reach into the defended areas and bring the civil population under bombardment. At La Fère, for example, the garrison were chiefly Gardes Mobiles ; the Prussian artillery moved up twenty-two guns and mortars, and after investing the place for nine days began a sharp bombardment which brought surrender the following day. At Thionville a force of 158 pieces of artillery was brought up, and the town bombarded for 58 hours, at the end of which the French garrison were so occupied in fire-fighting in the town that they could no longer attend to the defence, and forthwith surrendered.

One of the most interesting actions was that at Belfort. This was an extremely complex fortress constructed around Vauban's Third System, to which three more modern forts and two redoubts had recently been added. The garrison was some 1700-strong and the defence was commanded by Colonel Denfert of the Corps de Génie, who had had the best part of three months from the outbreak of war in which to organise the defence. The Prussians, after investing the place, spent three weeks preparing and then began the siege by driving in the French outposts from the surrounding villages, a task which turned out to be less simple than they had expected. Having assessed the defence, the besiegers began to move against the two redoubts ; these were simple works, roughly rectangular, with bomb-proof shelters and, most useful feature of all, very deep ditches cut in rock. Each redoubt had a collection of sixteen to twenty field guns and about a dozen mortars, and these were handled extremely skilfully, being frequently moved about inside the work so that the besiegers were unable to make a positive location and bring them under fire. Their ability to make life unpleasant for the attackers was most marked, particularly the high-angle fire of the mortars, and it is all the more remarkable when one considers the Prussian gun strength arrayed against them — 268 pieces. The earthen ramparts fully substantiated the results found in America, absorbing Prussian fire without much damage being done, and the attack had to resort to the sap and parallel.

The ground was hard and progress slow, and after a few days of digging the decision was taken to mount an assault from the first parallel ; it was a costly failure. One redoubt, the Haute Perche, had prepared its surroundings with primitive abattis, felling trees and placing entanglements of wire among the fallen and jagged branches and

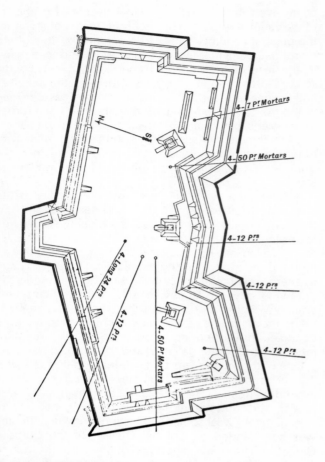

4 – 7 P.r Mortars

4 – 50 P.r Mortars

4 – 12 P.rs

4 – Long 24 P.rs

4 – 12 P.rs

4 – 12 P.rs

4 – 50 P.r Mortars

4 – 12 P.rs

The Basse Perche Redoubt at Belfort, typical of the detached works of the time, which stood punishment rather better than some of the more elegant permanent forts.

trunks; this sufficed to check the assault, which was then repulsed by musketry and case-shot fire. The other redoubt, Basse Perche, was reached by the assaulting troops, who managed to occupy the ditch; but once in, they could not scale the rock walls before being either killed or captured. The Prussians returned to their picks and shovels, and after another twelve days' labour their saps crowned the glacis in front of the redoubts.

Now comes the incredible part; when the Prussian troops debouched from their sapheads to cross the ditches and assault the Haute Perche redoubt, it was occupied by a guard of ten men who were found seated in one of the bomb-proof shelters. It was the Malakov Tower all over again, but this time with the French at the receiving end. The Basse Perche redoubt was somewhat more forcefully manned, but resistance was soon overcome and within a matter of minutes both positions were in Prussian hands. These two 'provisional works' — the official description — had withstood a siege of ninety-eight days, and now the Prussian troops were faced with the massive complexities of Vauban, four successive lines of work to be reduced before reaching the citadel. It might be reasonable to expect that, if a single ditch

and redoubt had taken so long, the besieging of the major work was going to be an interminable business. But it was all over in five days.

The Prussians immediately occupied the two redoubts with as many guns as they could pack inside comfortably, some sixty or more, and began pushing forward saps towards the first crownwork; that was sufficient for the garrison of Belfort, and without even waiting for the bombardment to begin they surrendered on the 103rd day of investment.

The siege of Paris was a longer (131 days) affair but it appears not to have been pushed with great urgency, the Prussians being satisfied to set down their siege train and open a bombardment; one of their problems being the supply of ammunition, since their advance had over-strained the Army supply system. It was not until a civil contractor was brought in that the movement of ammunition from Germany to the Paris siege train was sufficient to provide for a prolonged shelling. The course of the bombardment is not of interest here, but what emerges is that while the permanent works such as Issy suffered considerable battering, a number of provisional works thrown up immediately before the siege began proved to be incredibly difficult for the Prussians to deal with. The majority of these earthworks were gun batteries, mostly well masked and employing high-angle fire, and they were difficult enough to locate, let alone engage effectively. Indeed, it was realised after the siege that where guns were mounted in a prominent permanent work, they were usually well punished; Issy, for example, mounted forty guns and mortars of which seventeen were more or less damaged by quite random fire. Yet the batteries set down outside permanent works and concealed with even the minimum amount of skill were almost untouched.

The aftermath of 1870 was, as a result of the half-digested lessons leavened by the still-powerful grip of the geometrical school, a peculiar compromise between field works and masonry. Serre de Rivière, the French engineer, and Brialmont the Belgian, took to a policy of burying everything possible and relying on turrets to deliver the fire necessary both to deal with an enemy at a distance and protect the immediate environs of the work from assault. They both revealed a faith in fire-power which was grossly optimistic and entirely unfounded, and they both fell into the misapprehension that if a work were provided with cannon of *x* centimetres calibre, then it need only be proof against the effects of the same calibre. The Brialmont forts are outstanding examples of this erroneous belief.

As we have seen, the 1880s saw the arrival of the cupola and iron armour; they also saw the arrival of high explosives and their slow assimilation into military use as a form of filling for artillery shell. This in turn led to the question of what effect a high explosive shell would have on fortifications, and numerous trials were put in hand in various countries to try and reach some conclusions. It must be appreciated, at this point, that there is a considerable difference between 'high' and 'low' explosives, and their effect on structures is so different as to warrant these initial doubts on the part of the soldiers. To the layman it probably sounds so obvious to use high explosive for demolishing things, that such debates and trials as went on appear to confirm the presence of the dead hand of reaction; but there was — and is — rather more to it.

The difference between low and high explosives is very basic; a low explosive burns away — rapidly, it is true, almost instantaneously, but nevertheless its action is that of burning. In doing so it liberates gas, and this gas, expanding, performs some sort of work; such as propelling a shell from a gun. A high explosive, on the other hand, does not burn, but detonates — undergoes molecular disruption and chemical recombination. This also produces gas; but the speed of action is vastly different. An explosion, as of low explosive, travels at about 300 metres per second at atmospheric pressure; whereas a detonation of high explosive has a disruptive wave moving at 3000 metres a second or more. As a result of all this, the slow expansion of gas from a low explosive tends to exert a slow, 'lifting' effect, while the sudden expansion from a high explosive produces a shattering effect.

It follows from this that the results produced by a detonating high explosive shell — shattering the casing to produce lethal fragments — are not entirely compatible with those features of an explosive likely to make it a useful demolition charge — *i.e.* the slow and powerful heaving or lifting effect. It was this basic difference which led to debate and trial. Moreover, at that stage of explosive development the problem had an even more basic aspect; it was simply a question of finding a high explosive which was docile enough to tolerate being fired out of a gun at high velocity.

The dynamites and blasting gelatines were far too sensitive to withstand the violent accelerations involved, and eventually picric acid was adopted, under various names such as Lyddite, Melinite, or Shimose, as the standard shell filling. Probably the most significant experiments of the time were those performed at Fort Malmaison, near Soissons, in 1886 by the French, using 21-cm. Melinite-filled shells against various parts of the structure, some the original masonry works and some having been erected or modified for the trial. The damage done was quite extensive and the results seemed quite conclusive to the French. Yet on the other side of the Channel the British Army were not entirely convinced that a Lyddite-filled shell was any more effective in the fortress-breaking role than had been a gunpowder-filled one; and for once, they were right. The slow action of gunpowder was more appropriate for demolition than the rapid action of picric acid, but the great problem lay in applying it where it was wanted — underneath the work. Impact fuzes in the nose of the shell detonated the shell as soon as it struck; even without a fuze at all, a gunpowder-filled shell tended to burst as soon as the shell struck, due to internal friction. Picric acid, on the other hand, was less sensitive to this shock on arrival, and the solution eventually arrived at was to produce a hard-pointed shell carrying picric acid, and fit a fuze into the

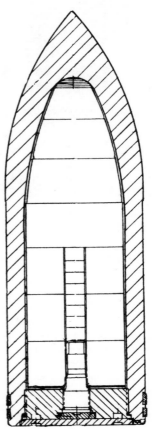

A piercing shell, showing the hard and thick tip, the base fuze and the relatively small explosive content.

base, where it was protected from damage on impact and where it could incorporate a short delay which would allow the shell to penetrate into the work before detonation.

But however it was looked at, the explosive shell was still a potent factor, and Brialmont, Mougin, de Rivière, von Sauer and other engineers and Professors of Fortification had to revise their ideas. As a first premise they took the 21-cm. howitzer shell as the article to be beaten, refusing to contemplate the possibility of a more powerful weapon ever being made sufficiently mobile to be considered a factor in siege warfare. While this may seem to be a short-sighted attitude, one must remember that the basic proviso of any field weapon of that time was that it had to be capable of being taken into action behind a team of horses, and this more or less automatically governed the maximum calibre. Nevertheless, there had been sufficient attempts in the past to develop heavy mobile ordnance to have given rise to reasonable doubt as to the wisdom of making such an assumption. The U.S. Federal forces had brought a 13-in. mortar into action near Richmond, mounting it on a railway truck, and it would have been a relatively easy task to lay a line of railway into the operational zones of France and Belgium,

Mallet's 36-in. Mortar, proposed for use in the Crimea. It was not built in time for use in the war, was completed afterwards, fired for trials and then abandoned.

given the density of railways in Europe by 1886. Moreover a Mr Mallet, in England, had proposed a 36-in. mortar in 1855 for service in the Crimea, and indeed two of these weapons were actually built. They could be transported piecemeal and fired shells weighing up to 2945 lbs with remarkable accuracy and devastating effect. (One of these mortars can be seen today outside the Royal Artillery barracks in Woolwich.) So there were poor grounds for assuming that 21 centimetres was the greatest practicable calibre; none the less, the assumption was made.

De Rivière, in the French works, adopted M. Mougin's idea of a concrete redoubt or keep, armed with turret guns, and enclosed by a ditched polygonal trace. The heart of the work was a concrete two-storied structure containing accommodation, and stores, and buried beneath 18 feet of earth. The roof of one metre of concrete was surmounted by a metre of sand, then a further metre of concrete, and then the earth cover. The theory behind this was that any projectile penetrating the earth would be checked by the upper layer of concrete and detonated, the sand layer acting as an additional shock absorber to prevent the effect of the detonation being transmitted to the inner skin of the keep. From this central keep tunnels ran to turrets, usually Mougin's retractable models, and to counterscarp galleries at the angles of the ditch. The gorge was closed by a form of tenaille which flanked the rear faces, while the glacis was extensively prepared with mines and wire entanglements.

As a result, the only visible feature from a distance was a grassy mound with one or two turret roofs flush with the surface. On the face of it, a sound design; but its efficiency as a fighting machine was questionable, since the usual armament consisted of a turret containing a 155-mm. gun, one or two turrets with 75-mm. guns, and two or three turrets with machine guns and searchlights. This was a vast reduction in gun power from that considered advisable in previous years, and was largely due to an unwarranted optimism in the efficiency of quick-firing guns. While these forts were being prepared, the 75-mm. Model of 1897 field gun was developed; with a highly effective recoil brake, a rapid-acting breech mechanism and a fixed, one-piece, round of ammunition, its aimed rate of fire as a field gun was in excess of fifteen rounds a minute, and mounted firmly in a turret it might well be expected to do even better. Thus the assumption arose that one quick-firer delivering fifteen rounds a minute was as good a proposition as five older guns firing at three rounds a minute each. As far as the amount of metal launched was concerned, this was true, but what the argument overlooked was that five guns could engage five different targets, while a single gun could only deal with one. Similarly, the sole 155-mm. gun was a potent weapon but while it was dealing with one besieging battery, half a dozen others could be trying to deal with it.

General Brialmont's creations were in similar vein, though throwing even greater reliance on the turret gun. However, he did make one considerable change in the basic architecture of the work in his treatment of the ditch, though it was not until the perfection of quick-firing artillery and machine guns that he incorporated it.

His original concept followed the principles of Mougin fairly closely, even carrying them to excess. His central redoubt was a four-tiered subterranean work surmounted by cupolas and connected by tunnels to caponiers and gorge face. His ditch was without scarp or counterscarp walls except at the foot, and even these walls were more in the nature of revetments to hold the earth. From the top of these walls the sides of the ditch sloped back to the glacis on the outside and forming a rampart on the inner side. At the foot of the rampart there was also a detached wall forming a species of chemin des rondes, the precise function of which has defied rational analysis ever since.

Outside the ditch the glacis sloped away and then rose again to form a terreplein on which open batteries could be mounted in time of need. The contour then fell to form a parapet for musketry, and finally fell once more to a second detached wall surmounting a ditch of classical form, walled on both faces and provided not only with counterscarp galleries but with casemates and galleries in the escarp communicating via tunnels with the terreplein level.

However admirable Brialmont may have thought this design, he was sufficient of a realist to change it for something better when the power of the high explosive shell became apparent. In 1888 he began the culminating work of his life, the chain of twelve forts surrounding Liège, and the works he produced there were probably the highest point of the fortress engineer's art. The trace was reduced to the most simple form, a triangle or trapezoid, and the principal feature was a monolithic concrete redoubt surmounted by up to eight turrets mounting 12-cm., 17-cm. or 21-cm. guns. This was sur-

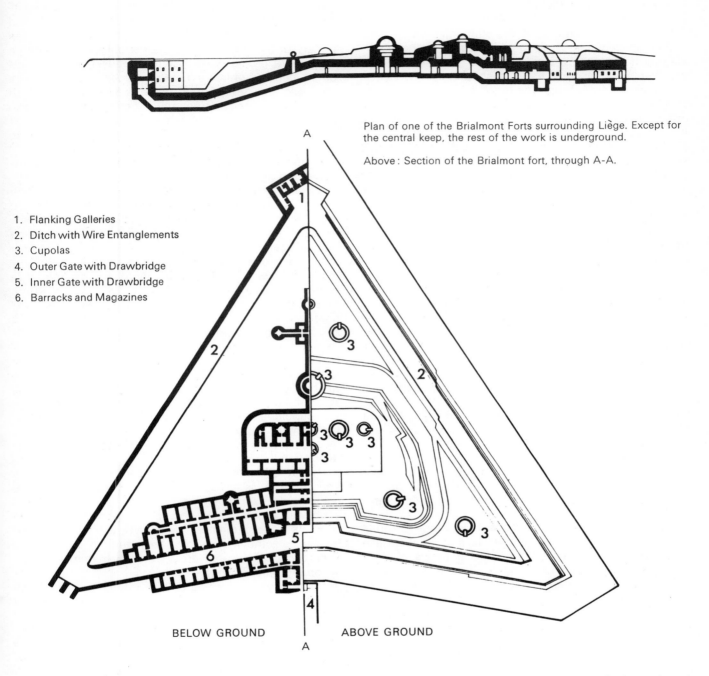

Plan of one of the Brialmont Forts surrounding Liège. Except for the central keep, the rest of the work is underground.

Above: Section of the Brialmont fort, through A-A.

1. Flanking Galleries
2. Ditch with Wire Entanglements
3. Cupolas
4. Outer Gate with Drawbridge
5. Inner Gate with Drawbridge
6. Barracks and Magazines

BELOW GROUND   ABOVE GROUND

rounded by a ditch and musketry parapet, and outside this ditch, though still within the trace, were other cupolas mounting light quick-firing guns for close defence, connected to the redoubt by tunnels.

Beneath the redoubt, a lower level, forming the accommodation and stores, ran back to the gorge face, terminating there in casemated galleries, while more tunnels passed beneath the main ditch to counterscarp galleries. A drawbridge crossed the ditch to a small outwork forming the gatehouse to the main entrance, and once again a drawbridge over a pit closed this when needed.

So far there was nothing exceptional; but when it came to the front face of the work, Brialmont introduced his unique feature. Instead of the ditch having perpendicular sides, the escarp sloped gently back from the floor of the ditch to the crest of the central redoubt, so that the turret guns had a perfect field of fire right into the ditch. The counterscarp wall was revetted and provided with galleries at the front angles, while the ditch floor was filled with entanglements and an 'unclimbable' steel palisade fence was sunk in concrete in the centre.

Although Brialmont still placed an unwarranted amount of reliance on a handful of ordnance, as long as the fort had a garrison capable of taking up position on the parapet, and especially if they were provided with a sufficiency of machine guns and ammunition, it seemed highly unlikely that such a work could be taken by assault. If the attackers crowned the glacis and gained the ditch, they no longer had a reasonably secure shelter; they would be confronted with 20 metres or so of entanglements, plus the 'unclimbable' fence, and for the entire time they would be exposed to small arms fire from the parapet and counterscarp galleries and close-range shrapnel fire from the turret guns. Brialmont had, it seemed, achieved a storm-proof work.

Unfortunately, as has often been pointed out, the tenure of a work largely depends on the morale of the occupants, and while the Liege forts were drawn up on plans which satisfied any imaginable tactical demand, they fell a good deal short when it came to considering the welfare of the occupants. An early critic had pointed out some of the possible defects arising from considerations of morale after a bombardment: 'The temptation to emerge, in order to spread out over a tumbled slope turned towards the enemy would not be specially strong . . . and 'The time and difficulty of filing the men out of dark and narrow underground passages and spreading them along the line they are intended to hold, or of getting them under cover again when the besieger's artillery opens fire, may easily be imagined.'

Moreover there were more fundamental criticisms of the internal arrangements. The latrines, for example, were in the counterscarp galleries, which meant a long walk when nature called, a peregrination not always convenient in the heat of action. As one fortress commander later said, 'Brialmont's military genius had an academic bent and he forgot that his works were made for human beings; he left out of account a natural function which does not cease during a bombardment — quite the reverse.'

Brialmont's involvement in the Liège forts is quite well known; what is less known is that he was also responsible for a chain of similar works around Bucharest. At that time (1885) the borders of Roumania were somewhat different than they are today; the Eastern frontier was so open that a Russian army could have moved in and taken Bucharest in a few days, while the Transylvanian Alps were the only obstacle to invasion from Austro-Hungary. Bucharest was therefore selected, as being the centre of commerce and government as well as the focal point of communication, to be turned into a place of arms within which the entire military strength of the country could be gathered. This, it was argued, would enable a defence to be offered and time gained in which any allies could come to the country's aid. Once this decision was taken, Brialmont was retained as an adviser and asked to produce designs.

His proposal was for a line of eighteen large forts at about four kilometres interval, supported by intermediate batteries; this is an interesting viewpoint since he set his face most firmly against any intermediate batteries in the chain of works around Liège. The forts were to be much the same as the Belgian pattern; a central redoubt with turreted guns and howitzers, surrounded by a ditch with detached wall and counterscarp galleries. There was also to be an open battery of four howitzers in the central redoubt, and he included a project for a parapet between redoubt and ditch, behind which a railway track would allow a 'movable shielded battery' to be moved from place to place to meet threats from any direction. In his designs, Brialmont expressed a preference for the cupolas of M. Mougin, as built by the St Chamond company in France, but once the intention of constructing the first was published, the Gruson company urged consideration of the Schumann designs, and as a result a competitive trial was held in December 1885 and January 1886.

By this time the two companies had made many trials, and their designs had been modified in the light of the experience they had gained. Gruson had abandoned chilled cast iron and now constructed his cupola of 'compound plate', 10 centimetres of wrought iron carrying on its face a 3-centimetre layer of soft steel and a 7-centimetre layer of hardened steel. Two 15-cm. Krupp breech-loading guns were mounted in the turret, the chase of the gun being formed into a rounded section so as to engage with a socket formed on the inner side of the turret plates, while the gun breeches rested in an arc-like structure of steel running between the roof and the floor. In this way the entire recoil force of the guns was transmitted directly to the turret structure and absorbed by banks of springs between the cupola and the surrounding glacis plate. Finally, the whole cupola could be retracted by a screw mechanism for about 6 inches, so that the roof plate rested solidly on the glacis.

The St Chamond design was considerably different. The cupola was a vertical-sided cast-iron structure 18 inches thick, supported by a hydraulic ram; its lower edge was protected by a cast-iron glacis anchored in concrete. The armament was two 155-mm. breech-loaders, electrically fired by an ingenious but grossly impractical system and provided with hydraulic recoil-absorbing mechanism.

The trial was performed by having the two competing cupolas erected and then engaging them with one Krupp and two French guns of the same type as were installed inside the structures, fired at various ranges to determine both the ease of hitting the cupolas and the effects of various patterns of piercing shells. By and large, the trial was not well performed; the conditions were such as to favour the French turret, while both the manufacturers had staffs of engineers and mechanics on hand to rectify any defect; the inventors of the turrets were also present, giving advice and directions whenever they felt so inclined. In spite of this, the trials showed the great advantage of the 'turtle-back' Gruson turret in deflecting or absorbing blows, while the trial ended just in time to save the face of M. Mougin. An English observer noted that the damage to the upper edge of his turret wall was so great that one more shell would have stripped off the roof like the lid of a sardine tin.

The results of the trial were never officially announced

The St Chamond Mougin turret, as proposed.

but it seems that Brialmont's inclination to the St Chamond company was sufficient to turn the scale in their favour. In the following year Mougin produced a new design which adopted the turtle-back profile of the Schumann pattern as well as the steel-faced plate construction, while retaining the hydraulic pivot and introducing some other small refinements, and this appears to have been the pattern adopted for the armament of the Bucharest line; unfortunately there seems to have been little information ever made public about its subsequent construction. However, similar works were built in other parts of Roumania, notably in a second 'place of arms' at the foot of the Carpathians near Kronstadt (later Brasov, later still Orasul Statin) and some works defending the more important crossings of the Danube. One of these latter, at Turtukai, was roughly handled by Mackensen in 1916, and photographs of the wreckage indicate the Gruson cupola was used here. The Bucharest position, however, was abandoned without any show of resistance in the face of the German advance in late 1916 and never showed its worth at all.

In the few years remaining to the fortress engineers before the world went mad, there were two other major works built which are worthy of notice, since they represent an interesting divergence of views. In the Far East the European powers had been occupied in carving out 'spheres of influence'; in 1898 the Russians signed a lease on the town and harbour of Port Arthur and began fortifying it; the Germans, at the same time, leased Kiaochow from the Chinese, and the British leased Weihaiwei. In all these, work began on preparing defences. In Weihaiwei it might have reached the dizzy height of a brace of 4.7-in. guns, but even that is doubtful. In the German and Russian possessions, however, the fortress engineers were given their head.

The works at Port Arthur have been described as inspired by Todleben' but as that master had been dead for fourteen years, his inspiration was rather nebulous. Its engineers were doubtless trained by Todleben, and it became apparent that they had learned little since. The works they produced were on a par with the French designs of 1840 or the Poznan works of the same period. A ring of forts was planned to completely surround Port Arthur on the landward side, while powerful coast batteries at each side of the harbour entrance completed the ring of defence. These coast batteries were the first to be built, and were undoubtedly efficient. For the most part they were simple open batteries on the cliffs, secure from naval gunfire by virtue of their high site, and these were supplemented by shielded quick-firing gun batteries at water-level to deal with torpedo-boat attacks. Liberal use of electric lights and controlled minefields rendered that quarter secure.

The landward defences, though, were slow to take shape. Six major forts and eight lesser intermediate works were planned, but finance, supply and labour problems prevented the completion of the line. The

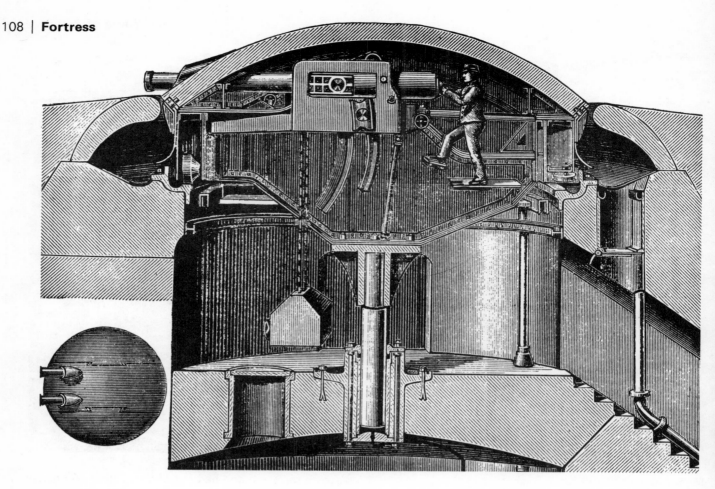

The Mougin turret, as adopted for the Bucharest works.

general form of the works was to a polygonal trace with casemated accommodation, guns in open batteries on the ramparts, ditches with caponiers and counterscarp galleries. The glacis were cleared to give good fields of fire, and wire entanglements were provided in some cases, but there was an astounding absence of concrete, armour plate, turrets or any other of the many newer additions to defensive strength which were, by this time, commonplace in the West. Since the Russians were by no means ignorant of these innovations, one can only assume they had fallen into the trap of over-confidence; the only enemy they were likely to have to deal with were the Japanese or Chinese, and they held neither of these in much esteem. Therefore, their reasoning seems to have run, 'the works to be built here need not be so technically advanced – and hence as expensive – as those that would be needed were a western power the threat.'

Across the sea at Tsingtao, in the new German city being built on the Kiaochow concession, there was no such under-estimation, and fortification there took on a totally different aspect. At first, the defences were simply a few open coast batteries to cover the harbour and its approaches, but in 1902 Japan and Britain signed a Treaty of Alliance which threatened to isolate Tsingtao in the event of war. Immediately the engineers were called

in and massive defensive works were begun. Four concrete forts, based more or less on Brialmont's theories, were built on high ground on the neck of the peninsula, so located that they could function equally well as coast or land defences. The intervals and flanks were occupied by open batteries of 105-mm. and 155-mm. guns, while the forts were provided with 15-cm. and 24-cm. guns and the central work, Fort Bismarck, with an additional two 28-cm. howitzers. All the fort guns were in the latest pattern of Krupp (who had acquired the Gruson company in 1893) cupolas, turtle-back armoured turrets mounting single guns and sunk into reinforced concrete redoubts.

This took care of the naval threat, as well as being a powerful land front, but the forts were too close to Tsingtao for comfort, and an outer line of redoubts was now built, six concrete works with field artillery and machine gun positions and with bomb-proof accommodation. Between these ran a defensive line of machine gun pill-boxes and fire trenches, and a line of reserve trenches was cut in the rear complete with dugouts and shelters. Finally, 200 yards in front of the redoubts, a scarped ditch was dug across the peninsula from coast to coast, the bottom being strewn with barbed wire, chevaux-de-frise and trous-de-loup; on the country side of the ditch a wall 6 feet high was built, and a 200-yard zone in front of this wall was sown with land mines, an electric fence being wired with contacts so as to fire mines in the vicinity of any attempt to cross it.

Chapter Six

The Testing Time

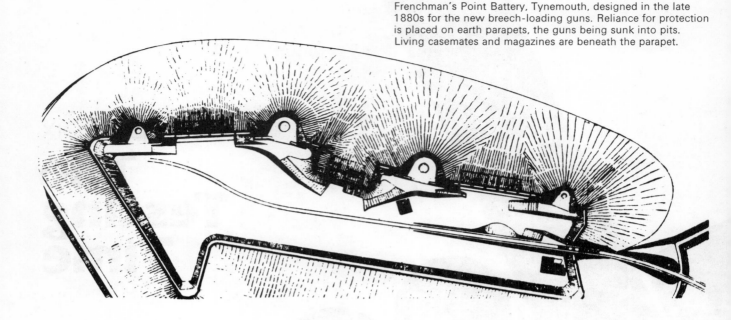

Frenchman's Point Battery, Tynemouth, designed in the late 1880s for the new breech-loading guns. Reliance for protection is placed on earth parapets, the guns being sunk into pits. Living casemates and magazines are beneath the parapet.

At the dawn of the twentieth century permanent fortification had reached its zenith. Countless millions of pounds, dollars, marks, francs, roubles and less well known currencies had been transmuted into concrete, steel and masonry erections of greater or lesser complexity across the face of the globe. No country it seemed, was so poor or backward as not to be able to afford a fortress of some sort, and the richer countries stinted nothing. England spent £12,154,416 between 1860 and 1890 on coast defences, plus £5,484,810 for the necessary guns to go inside the works, and in 1895 the first of a series of 'Naval Works Acts' was passed, authorising the construction of defences for naval bases throughout the Empire which, by 1901, totalled another £27,502,000. In the United States the Endicott Board of 1888 recommended construction costing over $126,000,000, though it must be hastily said that this enormous figure was rapidly pruned and never reached. How much treasure had gone into France's defences, the Belgian forts, the German and Austrian fortresses in Poland, the Bucharest forts, the Italian and Spanish coast defences, Heligoland, Kronstadt, will probably never be computed but it can only be in the thousands of millions of pounds. And now the bills were going to be called due; for while the fortress builders had been active, the artillerymen had been active too.

The first sign appeared much earlier than is commonly supposed, but it went unrecognised by almost everyone. In 1893 Chicago held its Columbian Exposition in Jackson Park, and as was normal practice in those days, manufacturers of every sort assembled there to display their products, the marvels of contemporary technology. One of the items on display was a 30.5-cm. (12-in.) calibre coast defence howitzer manufactured by the firm of Friedrich Krupp of Essen. Krupp was always appearing at exhibitions with huge cannon or immense lumps of steel or slabs of armour plate, in order to demonstrate how far in advance of his competitors he was, but, rather like the futuristic 'cars of tomorrow' seen at present-day automobile shows, everybody knew that these exhibits were no more than evidences of technical ability, and nobody ever credited them with having practical application.

Nobody but Krupp, that was; he knew full well that what he was exhibiting was soundly practical, if only armies could be persuaded to think about them. But although Krupp was doing his best to point the way, the first moves came from a totally unexpected quarter. In February 1904 Japan suddenly attacked the Russian Fleet at Port Arthur, and the Russo-Japanese War began.

Due to a combination of optimism, lethargy, scarcity of material and labour and insufficient money, the planned defences of Port Arthur had not been completed. As well as several small intermediate works, two major forts had never even been begun; but with a fair-sized field army to hold off the Japanese advance, there was ample time to prepare earthwork defences such as had proved their worth at Sebastopol, and with the Russian Far Eastern Fleet in the harbour and ample coast defence, there was no reason for undue alarm. Unfortunately, while the opportunity was there, the ability to make use of it was absent. The Commander of the Military District was Stossel, a martinet occupying a position far above his capabilities and whose military knowledge appears to have been encompassed between the covers of the Drill and Dress Manuals. Instead of completing the planned line, Stossel ordered the construction of a rampart and ditch around the town of Port Arthur, some 2000 yards *behind* the line of works. Since he was not the sort of man given to explanations, we do not know what possessed him to do this, but the materials and labour expended on this fruitless task could have been

Above: American 12-in. coast guns on disappearing carriages, Fort Monroe. Ammunition supply from underground magazines to lifts in the traverses between each gun. Protection is by a massive earth parapet in front, together with the concrete and masonry terreplein. *J. A. Wilson.*

Below: Another form of protection used by the US Coast Defence was to sink their high-angle mortars into deep concrete-lined pits; the magazines are on the same level as the floor of the pit and protected by the enormous thickness of earth between the mortar positions.

put to far better use; the inhabitants of the town appear to have had few illusions about its effectiveness, since they labelled it 'Stossel's Folly'.

Eventually, after a series of advances facilitated by inept Russian tactics, the Japanese invested Port Arthur in August 1904. The Japanese commander, General Nogi, was under some pressure from his War Department, since the Japanese Navy were concerned at the threat of the remainder of the Russian Fleet sailing

from the Baltic, joining up with the Far Eastern Fleet, and between them clearing the seas of Japanese ships in short order, and thus the capture of Port Arthur and its installations and the destruction of the Russian Fleet blockaded therein was a matter of priority. Nogi therefore lost no time in ordering an infantry attack on the north-western forts on the night of 14th August.

This attack introduced two factors which had been added to the fortification side of the equation since the

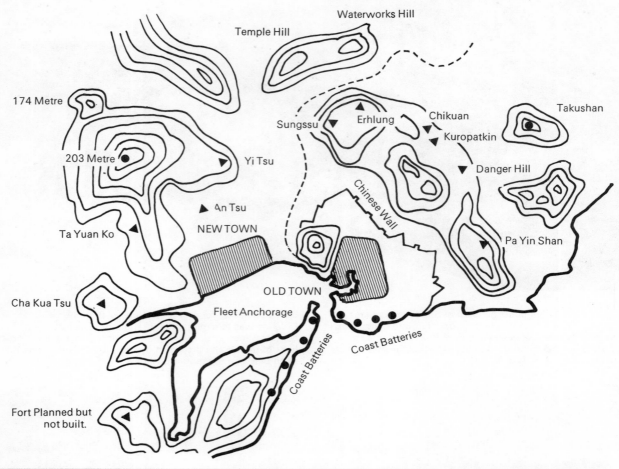

Waterworks Hill

Temple Hill

174 Metre

203 Metre

Yi Tsu

Sungssu   Erhlung   Chikuan   Takushan

Kuropatkin

An Tsu

Ta Yuan Ko

NEW TOWN

Danger Hill

Chinese Wall

OLD TOWN

Pa Yin Shan

Cha Kua Tsu

Fleet Anchorage

Coast Batteries

Coast Batteries

Fort Planned but
not built.

Above: The principal defences
of Port Arthur; numbers of
field works were placed on the
outlying hills after the war
began.

Left: One of the Russian coast
batteries at the siege of Port
Arthur. *Robert Hunt Library*.

war of 1870, the last in which major works had been involved: the machine gun and the barbed wire entanglement. The use of plain wire, stretched from pickets a foot or two above the ground, had long been advocated as a useful obstacle to place at the foot of the glacis to replace the abattis and trous-de-loup, and many fortresses employed this system; in the previous chapter we noted that Tsingtao used plain wire obstacles and connected them electrically to mines. Barbed wire, however, was relatively new; it first appeared in the agricultural world in the 1870s and only found its way into military manuals in the 1890s. The machine gun was equally an unknown quantity: the British Army had used Maxim, Gardner and Nordenfelt and Gatling guns in various minor campaigns in Africa and India with some effect, but their employment in quantity in major warfare was a matter of considerable speculation. None the less, from their earliest days, the possibilities of using them as a welcome addition to the fire-power of a fort or defensive post had been recognised; as early as 1863 the British Ordnance Select Committee, when reporting on the American Billingshurt-Requa Battery Gun, said of this class of weapon: 'They possess advantages which would render them valuable defensive instruments in musketry caponiers, flanking short ditches; and if adopted would save considerable expense in the construction of these works.'

The Japanese attack ran straight into both these devices. At the foot of the glacis of the works, barbed wire had been stretched between stakes in the standard fashion of the day: stakes four feet high and at intervals of six feet with wire stretched laterally and diagonally in five crossing layers. The forward troops began hacking their way into this, with the rear elements closing up, and when the whole lot were well involved with the wire, the Russians opened fire with their Maxim and Gorloff machine guns. (The Gorloff was the Russian name for the Gatling; they had been made in the U.S.A., but Colonel Gorloff, in charge of purchasing them, astutely had new nameplates made for the guns. Although generally obsolete by 1904, there were still large numbers in existence and they were quite adequate for fixed defences.) The guns had the range to an inch, and the result was a massacre.

On 16th August, Nogi sent in the customary emissary with a formal request for surrender, which was summarily rejected by Stossel, and after this the Japanese artillery set to work with 380 assorted guns and howitzers to shell the defences into silence. After a three-day bombardment another infantry attack was thrown in, and it was dealt with as summarily as the first; the two forts attacked were 1200 metres apart and were able to flank each other and cover all the intervening ground with fire. Over 15,000 Japanese were killed or wounded, and the only result was the capture of some field defences by a feint attack which had been almost ignored by the defence.

One of the factors which led Nogi to try these head-on tactics was the memory of the Japanese attack on Port Arthur ten years before, in the Sino-Japanese War.

Loading a Japanese 28-cm. howitzer at Port Arthur. *Radio Times Hulton Picture Library.*

But then the defence had been little more than a medieval wall poorly defended by a small garrison with bolt-action rifles, and the place was captured in half a day, with few losses. With such a precedent it was tempting to attempt to repeat the performance, but after two reverses Nogi had no choice but to fall back on the time-honoured system, send for his engineers and begin the first parallel.

However, he had something else up his sleeve. The Japanese Coast Artillery had a large number of 28-cm. howitzers, and some trials had revealed that it was perfectly feasible to dismount these, move them piecemeal on carts pulled by hundreds of coolies, and assemble them on ground platforms in the field. Eighteen of these howitzers had been removed from the fixed defences and loaded on to a transport ship, destined for Dalny, the Japanese-held port of supply near Port Arthur. Unfortunately for Nogi, the Russians had one of their few strokes of good luck when elements of their Vladivostok naval squadron came upon the convoy and, by sheer chance, sank the transport carrying the howitzers. Orders were immediately given for the preparation of another twelve equipments, and late in September they finally arrived in Dalny.

Being designed to drop their projectiles on to the decks of ironclads (since the armour there was lighter than on the sides), the howitzers were supplied with piercing shells as their primary projectile, and the result of these hard and pointed shells on concrete and masonry was something of a surprise, though, viewed from hindsight, there is no reason why it should have been. But the many experiments with guns against fortifications had invariably been done with common high explosive shell, or pointed, base-fuzed, but not specially hardened high explosive shell; either way the result was more spectacular than practical. But in the early 1900s the technique

of using a hard shell with a very small explosive charge and a base fuze against warships was beginning to be understood, and obviously a shell which could defeat armour plate might be expected to be efficient against concrete. And this proved to be the case at this first practical trial, the 28-cm. projectiles penetrating well into the defensive structure before detonating, where-

upon they blew large sections of concrete and masonry to dust.

For all that, Nogi's men still had to fall back on the tested and true methods of sapping and mining; by late October mine chambers had been excavated, and on the 30th a mine was fired beneath the ramparts of Fort Ehr-Lung-Shan. An artillery bombardment added to the confusion, and then an infantry assault was made. Once again the attack was repulsed with comparative ease; short-range shrapnel and machine gun fire swept the glacis, and the few survivors who reached the ditch were cut down by cross-fire from the caponiers and counterscarp galleries. It was of little use blowing a mine beneath the ramparts if the basic defensive fire-power was unimpaired.

Eventually, in late November, a prolonged attack on 203-Metre Hill and the intermediate works there gained a foothold; an observation post was set up and the 28-cm. howitzers were diverted from fortress shelling to bring their fire to bear on the anchored Russian fleet in the harbour. In spite of poor shooting — contemporary reports say that only thirty-six hits were obtained for 280 shells fired — the fleet was neutralised, the Japanese Navy placated, and Nogi could return to the reduction of the fortress. On 18th December mines behind the counterscarp and escarp of Chikuanshan Fort were fired, filling the ditch with rubble and allowing the assault parties to cross relatively quickly, scale the ramparts and enter the work. After eight hours of desperate fighting, the fort was in Japanese hands. Then, ten days later, a massive mine was detonated beneath the parade of Fort Ehr-Lung-Shan; as luck would have it, most of the garrison were assembled above the mine for roll-call when it was fired. The vast majority were killed instantly and the remainder were badly shaken and offered little resistance to the assault which followed. Finally Sungssu fort was mined, and once more the Japanese had a stroke of luck: the detonation of the mine set off the main fort magazine, and totally wrecked the work.

On 2nd January 1905 the Russians surrendered; the assault had cost the Japanese 57,780 casualties and the Russians 31,306, while the defence lasted 148 days. Had the defence been in the hands of a better soldier, and had the defensive works been properly organised during the early months of the war, then there is little doubt that the place could have held out much longer; but then, the same sort of thing could be said of a lot of sieges. The notable thing about it is that the Japanese had to force their way into every work they attacked and engage the garrison in hand-to-hand combat to achieve a result. The spacious days of yore, when the garrison surrendered with honour once the 'practicable breach' had been made — a practice seen as recently as 1870 when several French forts surrendered thus — such days were gone for ever. The other notable feature is the fact that Port Arthur was the last fortress to be taken by Vauban's system of saps and parallels; henceforth a more direct and brutal system was to take over, and it too could be said to have begun at Port Arthur.

As was common practice in those days, a number of foreign military observers attended the Russo-Japanese War to report to their own armies on tactics and new developments. Most of these officers appear to have dwelt principally on the handling of field artillery and the use of machine guns, but in the course of their reports several other nuggets could be discerned, and one which the

Krupp's 42-cm. 'Gamma' howitzer emplaced for testing at the Proving Ground at Meppen in 1911. The wheeled arch to the right is the erecting gantry. *Ian Hogg.*

BATAAN PENINSULA

Mariveles

Corregidor (Ft. Mills)

Caballo (Ft. Hughes)

Rosario

Mills : 18 x 12 in : 2 x 10 in : 5 x 6 in : 10 x 3 in Guns.
Hughes : 4 x 12 in : 2 x 14 in : 2 x 6 in : 2 x 3 in Guns.
Drum : 4 x 14 in : 4 x 6 in Guns.
Frank : 2 x 14 in : 8 x 12 in : 2 x 3 in Guns.

El Fraile (Ft. Drum)

Ternate

CAVITE PROVINCE

Carabao (Ft Frank)

Manila Bay, showing the location of the coast defence forts

German Army apparently fixed upon was the performance of the 28-cm. howitzers against fortifications. Should Germany decide to go to war, whichever way she moved, she would come up against fortresses, generally of the Brialmont pattern, with thick concrete and armoured turrets, and it was high time to begin trying to solve this problem with something more technically advanced than picks and shovels. Krupp were requested to look into the matter, and taking the 30.5-cm coast howitzer (which was code-named 'Beta'), they modified it so as to be capable of transportation in pieces on tractor-drawn trailers. The shell fired by this weapon weighed 800 lbs, and it was felt that its performance might be marginal against well-designed works. So a fresh design was begun, of a 42.0-cm. (16-in.) calibre howitzer called 'Gamma'. The man behind this was Professor Rausenberger of Krupps; and by 1911 'Gamma' had become a practical weapon. Much of the ballistic calculation was done by a Captain Becker, later to become internationally famous as a ballistician and to become the Director of Artillery Research for the Wehrmacht in the 1930s. The 'Gamma Morser' fired a 2200-lb shell to 15,530 yards, but the final design of the shell was a long and involved affair before a suitable pointed shell containing 310 lbs of TNT and a base fuze was perfected.

The only drawback to 'Gamma' was that it weighed 137.8 tons in action, and the only way it could be moved was to dismantle it by using a crane and carrying it piecemeal on ten railway wagons. If all went well the weapon could be off-loaded and assembled ready to fire in about 36 hours. This was far from satisfactory to the Army, so Rausenberger sat down at his drawing board once more. The barrel of the howitzer was reduced in length and the carriage re-designed and lightened, and the weight in firing order brought down to 42.6 tons. It could now travel by road in five loads and be assembled, using a light triangular gyn-hoist, in a few hours.

The shell weight had to be reduced to 1800 lbs and the range also came down to 10,250 yards.

The manufacture of these weapons — there were only two in existence when war broke out in 1914 — was conducted in such secrecy that beyond a handful of soldiers and Krupp employees their existence was entirely unknown, and it was not until war broke out that they were unveiled. But before we consider this unveiling, there was one more piece of fortification going forward which deserves mention because of its unique form.

In 1898 the Spanish-American War gave the U.S.A. the Philippine Islands, and in 1905 the National Coast Defense Board (the Taft Board) recommended fortifying Manila Bay and Subic Bay in order to protect the U.S. Naval Base to be established at Cavite. Major defences were put in hand from 1907 onwards with the construction of Fort Mills on Corregidor Island, Fort Hughes on Caballo Island nearby and Fort Frank on Carabao Island. This made two forts at the north side of the entrance to Manila Bay and one to the south, leaving a considerable gap through which ships could possibly slip under cover of darkness. A proposal was put forward to construct an artificial island somewhat on the lines of the English iron forts, and to use a tiny, existing island called El Fraile as a torpedo-launching station. In July 1908 a Lieutenant John J. Kingman (later to become Brigadier-General) of the U.S. Corps of Engineers wrote to the District Engineer in Manila and suggested that a cheaper and more effective solution might be to encase El Fraile in concrete and place upon it two Gruson-type cupolas, each with two 12-in. guns. His original plans bear a strong resemblance to some of Mougin's earlier ideas: between the two cupolas were five smaller ones to house observation instruments, as well as firing stations and control positions for torpedoes and controlled minefields.

'The Concrete Battleship'. *Ian Hogg.*

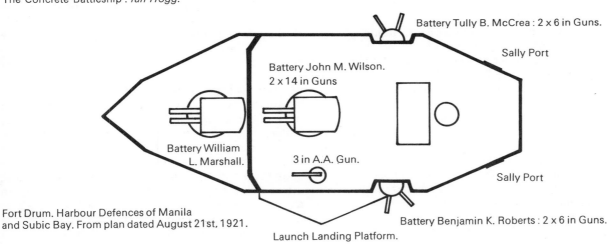

Battery Tully B. McCrea : 2 x 6 in Guns.

Sally Port

Battery John M. Wilson.
2 x 14 in Guns

Battery William
L. Marshall.

3 in A.A. Gun.

Sally Port

Fort Drum. Harbour Defences of Manila
and Subic Bay. From plan dated August 21st, 1921.

Launch Landing Platform.

Battery Benjamin K. Roberts : 2 x 6 in Guns.

The subsequent changes and discussions which took place need not concern us, but with remarkable rapidity Lieut. Kingman's idea was seized upon, modified, and put into effect. Instead of cast steel cupolas with 12-in. guns, armoured Naval-pattern turrets mounting two 14-in. guns each were installed, one at a higher level to be able to fire over its partner. The concrete casing of the island roughly followed the outline of the rock and was finally shaped very much like a warship, with a long tapering 'bow' and a blunt 'stern'. The resemblance was heightened by the provision of a lattice mast to carry searchlights and a depression position finder, so that very soon Fort Drum (its official name) became universally known as the 'Concrete Battleship'. With the exception of some emergency works on Hawaii during the Second World War, this was the only turreted fortification ever constructed by the United States, and it was in full commission by 1912.

Then, in 1914, Germany rode to war on the back of the famous Schlieffen Plan, which, in simple terms, meant a lightning thrust round the flank of the Franco-German border through Belgium to Paris in order to defeat the

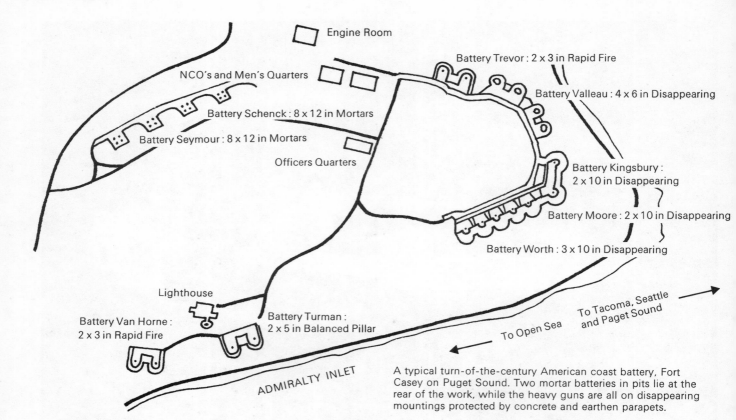

A typical turn-of-the-century American coast battery, Fort Casey on Puget Sound. Two mortar batteries in pits lie at the rear of the work, while the heavy guns are all on disappearing mountings protected by concrete and earthen parapets.

French before the slumbering Russian bear could complete mobilisation and take the field on the Eastern Front. This manoeuvre meant a head-on collision with Brialmont's works at Liège and Namur, but the German Army had taken the measure of these defences and thought that they would fall to a straightforward infantry assault.

Brialmont's forts were undergunned and badly sited to begin with; two 21-cm., two 15-cm. and half-a-dozen 75-mm. guns in turrets was normal armament, while the siting, which looked perfect on a map, in fact took little account of the intervening terrain, and there was a large amount of wooded ground and small folds out of observation of the forts. Brialmont had firmly refused to contemplate the building of intermediate works, affirming that the forts could provide all the protection needed. This mischief was compounded by rank bad staff work; when General Leman was appointed as commander of the Liège Fortress in May 1914, the Belgian General Staff actually refused to tell him how many troops he would have in the event of war, which rather stultified his planning, and he was expressly forbidden to construct any field earthworks in case such activity should offend the Germans. It was not until 29th July that this order was rescinded, and a reinforcing division arrived to flesh out the skeleton garrisons of the forts — a week before the German Army arrived.

The attempt at an infantry assault failed, as it deserved to; the Germans attempted to infiltrate between the works, but although much ground to the front was 'dead' to the forts; the intervening ground was well covered and the advance came to a bloody halt, trapped between the glacis of Forts Pontisse and Liers. Another assault was stopped by Fort Boncelles, and the Germans realised that, after all, even a poor fort can be an obstacle. The 42-cm. howitzers were sent for from the Krupp works where they were stored, but before they left Essen the first breach in the ring of forts was made by nothing more technologically advanced than a battery of ordinary 105-mm. field howitzers. Fort Barchon, to the north east of the town, was attacked by the German 27th Division on 8th August; more by way of morale-raising than with any hope of achieving significant results, the light howitzer battery firing a few rounds at the fort. As it so happened, troops of the 34th German Brigade were moving on the other side of the fort and a large number of the garrison had emerged to man the parapet on that side; the shells from the 27th Division took them in reverse, causing some thirty casualties, and this sudden attack from an unexpected direction so surprised the occupants of the work that the white flag was run up forthwith and the fort yielded without further ado.

On 12th August the 42-cm. howitzers were in position, and at 17.40 hours that evening one of them opened fire on Fort Pontisse. The first round landed some distance from the fort, throwing up an immense cloud of smoke and earth, and the garrison of Pontisse were convinced that the Germans were attempting to mine the work in the traditional manner and had somehow suffered a premature explosion. The garrisons of the surrounding forts were equally convinced that the magazine of Pontisse must have detonated. They had five or six minutes in which to discuss these beliefs, and then the second round fell, closer to Pontisse, to be followed by five more, all creeping closer. The eighth shell penetrated the three metres of concrete forming the roof of the central redoubt, penetrated into the interior passages, and detonated there. With that, the howitzer stopped firing for the night, leaving the occupants of Pontisse to worry about what the following day might bring.

Next morning both howitzers opened fire on Pontisse with devastating results. Captain Becker later related how he would pick up' the shell in mid-flight with his binoculars and watch it until it struck; this may sound an unlikely story, but it is perfectly possible, especially with such a large shell fired at a velocity of about 1200 feet per second and at a relatively short range. On one such occasion he saw the shell descend on one of the armoured cupolas; there was a vivid flash as steel met steel and then a pause while the projectile burrowed into the redoubt. Then the cupola erupted from its anchorage, being flung over one hundred feet away in two pieces. Subsequent examination showed that the shell had punched a hole clean through the armoured turret. The effects on concrete were even more spectacular; though a German engineer officer who later inspected the forts gave his opinion that the Belgian Army had been robbed by unscrupulous contractors. 'The concrete,' he reported, 'was as poor as it could be and still hold together.'

After four and a half hours of battering, the conditions in Fort Pontisse became intolerable. Armour was peeled away like cardboard, concrete pulverised into dust, huge blocks of masonry flung awry. The passages in the fort filled with dust and fumes which the ventilation systems totally failed to clear. At 12.30 the garrison surrendered, and the howitzers turned to Fort Embourg to repeat the performance. Embourg surrendered at 17.30. The next day saw the fall of Liers (09.40), Fleron (09.45), and the following day accounted for Boncelles (07.30) and Lantin (12.30). Chaudfontaine was somewhat more resistant and lasted until the following day at 09.00 when the magazine detonated — it is not entirely clear to this day what caused the detonation — and the resulting casualties and damage led to surrender.

This had made sufficient gaps in the defences of Liège to allow the army to move into the town and install the howitzers there so as to deal with the few remaining works which, on the west of the town, still formed an obstacle. Fort Loncin, in which General Leman had his headquarters, was the first to be brought under fire, and the nineteenth shell penetrated the magazine and detonated its contents, opening up the fort like a volcano. This appalling sight led the two remaining works, Hollogne and Flemalle, to surrender forthwith, and the Germans were masters of Liège.

The lessons of Liège were several; to begin with, it pointed to the fact that it was of little use to pontificate about the likely calibre of weapon to be brought against a work. Brialmont and his contemporaries had gambled on the 21-cm. howitzer being the maximum calibre suitable for field deployment; they had lost.

The second grave defect lay in the construction of the works; leaving aside the question of the quality of the concrete, it was now seen that the designs had been poorly thought out from the point-of-view of living and fighting in the works for a period of time. In Brialmont's time anything was good enough for soldiers, and as long as lip service was paid to the basic demands for ventilation, sanitation and water supply, honour was satisfied. An interesting comment on contemporary standards can be found in the Poznan forts, which, insofar as this aspect went, were of much the same class as Brialmont's: Fort VII was used by the Germans as a prison during the Second World War, and a pamphlet describing it, published by the Polish 'Organisation for the Preservation of Monuments', refers to the conditions in the casemates: 'The sanitation and hygiene conditions were terrible. No sunshine or fresh air ever penetrated to the dungeons in the dark vaults, which were running with damp, and were mouldy and smelly.' It may have been hell for a Polish prisoner in 1940 but it was home for a German soldier in 1885.

Another fault at Liège was that the water cisterns and pipelines were located so that the detonation of shells on the concrete, even where they failed to penetrate, caused sufficient vibration to crack open pipes and tanks and allow the water to leak away, either into the ground beneath the fort or into the works themselves, making life even more uncomfortable.

The tactical shortcomings were various; firstly the incredible refusal of Brialmont to countenance intermediate earthworks and detached batteries. Secondly his concentration on protecting the forward faces while relying on nothing more substantial than a masonry wall at the gorge, secure in the belief that the ring of works was inviolable and that no attack could develop from the rear. Thirdly, stemming from this, the siting of forts so that while they commanded ground on their immediate front and flanks adequately, they had practically no command at the rear.

One of the most outspoken critics of contemporary fortification at the turn of the century was Major G. Sydenham Clarke of the Royal Engineers, later to become Baron Sydenham. Although somewhat acid in his observations, even to the point of exaggeration, he was a knowledgeable man and his remarks were based on sound experience. Writing in 1893 on Brialmont's designs, Clarke made some comments which make interesting reading in the light of the events which took place at Liège:

'The slope at the rear of the infantry line would render it untenable under artillery fire, since all fairly accurate shells would be caught and burst at the men's backs . . .'
— precisely what happened at Fort Barchon.

'The *vive force* school proposes . . . to shell them heavily and then storm . . . If such a method of avoiding the delays occasioned by a siege is ever to prove successful, for forts proposed by General Brialmont are well calculated to facilitate it. A work designed on the principles of the Roman Catacombs is suited only for the dead in a literal or in a military sense. The mere lighting of the underground communications . . . will be a serious matter.'

The remains of a cupola at Fort Loncin, Liège. Notice
the construction of the iron glacis, in interlocking segments.
Robert Hunt Library.

The ring of forts surrounding Verdun

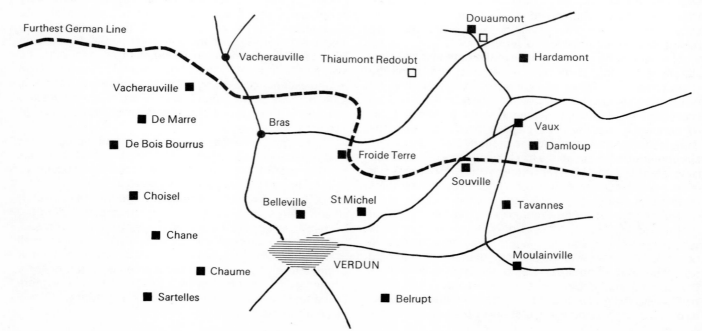

The Fort of Manonviller, France; bombarded by the 42-cm. howitzers on 26–27 August 1914, it capitulated with 700 men after 158 shots had been fired, some of the results of which can be seen here. *Robert Hunt Library.*

It would be pointless to describe in detail the performance of the numerous forts of Europe in the following four years, for with few exceptions the story is the same as that of Pontisse. The Austro-Hungarian Army was provided with a number of 30.5-cm. howitzers, highly mobile and tractor-drawn, which had a performance but slightly inferior to the German 42-cm. weapons. Forts on the Roumanian, Italian and Russian frontiers succumbed to the hammering of one or other type of ordnance with little delay. In one or two instances, though, things were not quite so easy for the attackers. At Tsingtao the Japanese brought out their 28-cm. howitzers once more, but the German concrete and armour was of infinitely better quality than the Belgian material and the damage done was negligable; the siege there had to run its proper course and it was not until the German defenders ran out of ammunition that Tsingtao fell.

The next batch of defences to come into prominence were the works of Serre de Rivière at Verdun. These had been begun in the late 1870s and were similar in conception to Brialmont's works, though more soundly constructed. They suffered from the same defects in being relatively poorly armed, but on the other hand they were excellently sited and liberally provided with intermediate redoubts and earthworks so as to form a really sound defensive line. Unfortunately, while they had not been so neglected as the Liège works, they had been somewhat discounted by the higher command. After seeing the rapid collapse of Liège, Namur, Maubeuge and other fortresses, the French GQG opined that (as Petain put it) 'the ideas of permanent fortification were permanently doomed. It was believed that forts, too conspicuous as targets, were destined to immediate destruction, and that only fieldworks, being less susceptible to attack by artillery, would offer . . . effective means of resisting the enemy's onslaughts.' As a result of this opinion the forts at Verdun (as well as many others away from the seat of operations) were largely stripped of armament in order to produce guns for the field armies, since there was a grave lack of artillery heavier than the ubiquitous 75-mm. field gun when the war broke out. All the ditch-flanking and caponier armament was removed and many of the smaller turrets stripped of their 75-mm. guns. Some forts were left with no armament at all, while those which did retain guns only did so because the heavier turreted weapons were impossible to remove without dismantling part of the fort to allow the cupola to be lifted out.

For a variety of reasons, all of which seemed good but some of which had more validity than others, the German Army decided to attack Verdun in strength, and one of the obstacles they would have to overcome would be some of the forts on the northern side of the city, notably Douaumont, Hardaumont, Vaux (which had been completely stripped of guns from top to bottom), Damloup, Froide Terre, Souville and Tavannes.

As a preliminary, the 42-cm. and 30.5-cm. howitzers had been brought up and had fired from time to time, but with surprisingly little effect. De Rivière's concrete and armour withstood the fearsome projectiles better than Brialmont's, and he had also been more ingenious in his construction. The 3-metre concrete roof of his redoubt was surmounted by an equal thickness of earth and sand, and a reconstruction in the early years of the century had added a 'burster course' of reinforced concrete, separated from the redoubt roof by over a metre of sand and intended to detonate projectiles before they reached the skin of the redoubt. Moreover, the firing of the giant howitzers was attended with some risk; one of the peculiarities of the 42-cm. was that it discharged an enormous and unique smoke ring into the air at each shot, and thus announced its presence to French artillery observers who immediately opened furious counter-battery fire on to it.

Since Verdun had been a 'quiet sector' for some time, the forts were inadequately manned, and last-minute preparations by the French, when they began to suspect the possibility of a German attack, were principally concerned with digging trench lines and wiring well ahead of the works. One fort, Hardaumont, was completely without a garrison, while the others were manned by small detachments of reservists, because it was believed that any German advance would be stopped well before it reached the defensive ring. But the German attack was much more ferocious than expected; it began at 07.15 with an artillery bombardment heard a hundred miles away and which continued until 16.00, when the infantry assault began. As a result, the German advance met with little initial resistance and penetrated much deeper into the French lines than had been expected; indeed, had the German troops been more enterprising, it would have gone a good deal further. Hence, the forts suddenly became the focus of attention. They dominated the skyline and inevitably, since the Germans assumed them to be fully armed and manned, they were approached warily by the assault.

One is tempted to turn again to Clarke for another percipient quotation: . . . it is conceivable that half a company led by some Dundonald could secure the easy capture of one of these masterpieces of pure theory.' This is exactly what happened at Fort Douaumont; the Dundonald in this case was one Sergeant Kunze, Pioneer Sergeant of the 24th Brandenburgers, and instead of half a company, he had a ten-man squad of pioneers. Kunze and his men had been attached to the leading infantry with the simple instruction to 'eliminate all obstacles in front of the infantry.' After dealing with various minor problems such as wire, Kunze found himself outside Fort Douaumont; this, obviously, was an 'obstacle in front of the infantry' and Kunze, in accordance with his orders, set about 'eliminating' it.

Douaumont was manned by an elderly sergeant-major and fifty-six reservist gunners, and was operating quite independently of the troops on the ground outside it. An incredible division of responsibility was the cause of this; the forts came nominally under the control of the Governor of Verdun, while the troops outside were part of XXX Corps. The Corps Commander had, so it is said, visited the fort before the battle began with a view to integrating it in the sector defence, but he was refused entrance by the sergeant-major on the grounds that the work was only responsible to the governor. The Corps Commander, incredibly, seems not to have pursued the point with the elderly concierge, but the question of responsibility was still being discussed when the storm broke, whereafter it was forgotten in the excitement. As a result, when Sergeant Kunze arrived at the ditch before Douaumont, the majority of the garrison were down in the redoubt, only one 155-mm. turret gun being manned; and this was firing in the opposite direction in a desultory fashion whenever the gunner's attention was drawn to something of interest.

Kunze's party cut their way through the glacis entanglements, entered the ditch, cut through more wire and were confronted with the 'unclimbable' fence at the foot of the escarp. After wandering along the ditch they found a gap in the fence, blown by a chance shell, passed through and eventually came to a caponier with a gun port — but no gun. Kunze formed his men into a human pyramid, clambered up and through the port, opened an outer door and, with a couple of men admitted, entered the redoubt. More by luck than good management he found the 155-mm. turret and captured the gun detachment at pistol point. He then found some twenty men of the garrison in a casemate and locked them in, after which Douaumont was no longer an effective section of the French defences.

By this time the lack of effective fire from the fort had attracted more German infantry, and very shortly the work was firmly secured. Among the first to arrive was a Captain von Brandis; he very astutely volunteered to go back and report the capture of the work, and in doing so he made sure that the tale lost nothing in the telling; he became the 'Hero of Douaumont' and poor Kunze and his ten pioneers were forgotten.

The works around Verdun were battered out of recognition in the ensuing months as the tide of battle raged back and forth. Douaumont was eventually recaptured, Vaux changed hands twice, Hardaumont fell (inevitably, since it was unmanned), Douaumont was lost again, Froid Terre was entered by the Germans but regained by the French, but on the whole these had ceased to be forts — they were mere names in a sea of mud and rubble, more objectives for infantry, and their designed functions no longer applied.

Coast fortification saw little action during the course of the First World War: the only major confrontation between ships and shore defences came in the Dardanelles. The straits were fortified by a number of antiquated forts of simple trace with a variety of guns mounted en barbette, supplemented by open batteries alongside. A group of four comparatively weak forts lay at the entrance; ten miles above, near Kephez, came a second group

Fort Douaumont after the battle; the casemates have been
severely battered by the concentration of German artillery fire
but are still habitable. *Imperial War Museum.*

The Turkish fort of Sedd-El-Bahr at the entrance to the
Dardanelles, a typical casemated water-level work with barbette
batteries on the ramparts above. *Robert Hunt Library.*

mounting four 15-cm. guns assisted by a collection of field guns and howitzers in open emplacements. The Narrows, where the channel closed in to only 1300 yards, was protected by a formidable array of guns from 35-cm. through 28-cm., 24-cm. and 21-cm. to 15-cm. in calibre. The first naval attack on the Dardanelles was in November 1914 when four elderly British and French battleships bombarded the outer works for a few minutes, for no seemingly very good reason.

In February 1915, in connection with the questionable attempt to broaden the scope of the war, force a passage to Russia and possibly convince the Turks of the error of their ways, an Allied fleet of eight armoured ships engaged the forts at the entrance at long range. The bombardment was continued for two days, and resumed some five days later, the batteries eventually being silenced. Naval and marine landing parties were sent ashore to complete the demolition of the works, and at first they met with little opposition and were able to place demolition charges on some fifty or more of the guns. (It is worth noting that the majority of the photographs which purport to show the damage to the works after the naval bombardment were actually taken after this shore party had finished their operations, and that the material damage to the guns and works by the shelling was relatively small.) But the Turks soon recovered from their initial surprise and subsequent attempts at landing were roughly handled.

From this high point the naval attempt degenerated into a fiasco which formed an appropriate overture to the whole Gallipoli nonsense. The minesweepers which should have cleared the channel to allow the fleet to proceed further and engage the works higher up the straits were manned by civilians who, upon being shot at from the shore, understandably complained and refused to go further unless the offending batteries were silenced. Replacing the civilian crews with naval personnel, the sweepers set forth at night and were then cut to pieces by short-range gunfire directed by searchlights.

Meanwhile the Turks harassed the fleet by using batteries of mobile howitzers which were moved from day to day, and made retaliatory fire worthless by deploying squads of men with pyrotechnic simulators which emitted flashes and bangs in a creditable imitation of artillery. Nevertheless, the Allied fleet, after further delay, finally advanced up the straits and when about eight miles south of the Narrows, began firing on the forts there with their heaviest guns. The magazine in one fort was fortuitously struck and detonated, but beyond that the damage inflicted was minimal. But then disaster struck; the Turks had laid fresh mines during the previous night, and the French battleship *Bouvet* now struck one and sank instantly. Two other ships were sunk shortly afterward, and three more so damaged that they had to be beached. The fleet withdrew, having suffered 750 casualties and having made little impression on the defences. All in all, it bore out Admiral Lord Fisher's original contention: 'No sailor but a fool attacks a fortress.'

On the Western Front the stalemate of trench warfare had brought the redundant art of field fortification into new prominence. Field fortification was largely considered as something done hurriedly in order to hold a position temporarily while reinforcements were brought up in order to resume the advance, or, at most, an extempore sort of work performed in order to defend a camp site during 'native wars'. Such works began with 'shelter pits', a foot deep and with the excavated earth thrown in front to make a slight parapet; moved on to 'rifle pits', $3\frac{1}{2}$ feet deep, 4 feet long and 5 feet broad, with a fire-step and parapet; and finally arrived at 'shelter trenches' which were graded as 'half-hour', 'one-hour' or 'two-hour' trenches according to the time available for excavation, and thus became wider and deeper, with loopholes and overhead cover. The official texts of the 1890s went on to outline methods of constructing loopholes, obstacles, stockades and a variety of other devices, largely intended for use in warfare against unsophisticated enemies with low-velocity weapons.

The first trenches excavated in 1915 were more or less in accord with these policies, since it took some time for the truth to sink in, that this was to be the battle line and that the war of movement was over. Gradually, with the acceptance of this fact, the combatants began to delve into the earth and, eventually, tempered by national characteristics and the adequacy of the supply organisations, the troops disappeared below ground.

The British and German policy was to establish a sound and solid front line and reinforce it from the rear, and they evolved a fairly common system of constructing a deep and wide trench, with a fire-step and loopholes, adding dug-outs here and there as living quarters, kitchens, first-aid stations and so forth. Since there was a danger of enfilade fire and another of mortar bombs and grenades, the trench was angled at short intervals and divided into sections or 'traverses', the word obviously coming from the similar reasoning which had placed traverses on the covered way. In front of the parapet, at some convenient distance, would be one or more thick belts of barbed wire with gaps here and there, covered by machine gun fire, to allow raiding parties to sally forth and return.

Some hundred or so yards behind this came the 'support trench', in which reinforcements for the front 'fire-trench' lived. This trench was often so sited that the occupants could bring rifle fire to bear over the heads of the occupants of the fire trench and thus help to break up any attack. The two lines were connected by zig-zag 'communication trenches', to allow supplies to be taken to the fire trench and also to allow the reinforcements to move forward when required. Later a third trench was introduced; the 'bombing trench', about twenty yards behind the fire trench; in this were dumps of hand grenades and a number of skilled bombers. In the event of a raid on the fire trench, their task was to throw bombs into the fire trench and thus break up the raid.

With this fundamental basis the trench systems then proliferated into the rear area for as great a distance as the constructors considered necessary for safety,

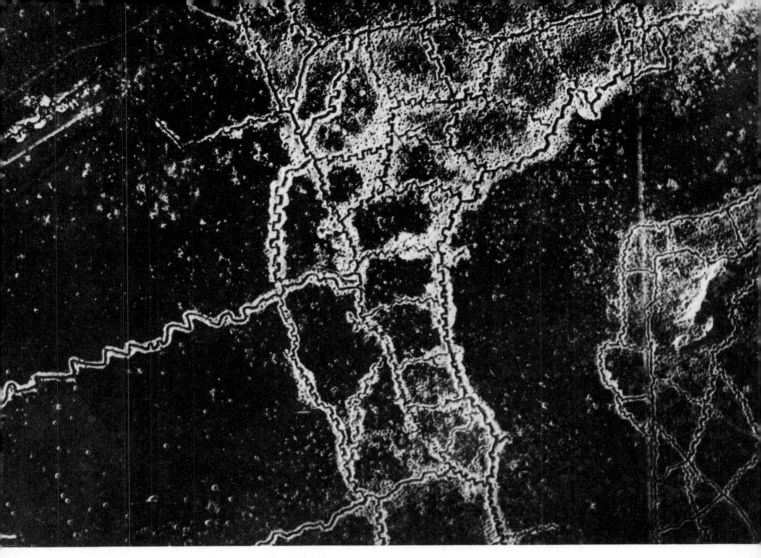

Aerial view of typical trenches in Flanders. The white outline is due to chalk spoil, and the traverses in the front line trench are easily distinguished. *Imperial War Museum*

Left: A German trench with a sniper taking aim. Notice the brushwood revetting and the screw pickets in the foreground for use in erecting barbed wire entanglements.

sometimes for miles, culminating in a 'GHQ' trench from which access to the 'outside world' was gained. And as the war progressed, so the trenches became more refined and better engineered; the greatest drawback, of course, was the same water-table problem which had led Coehorn to his Dutch System. As soon as one started to dig, water appeared; but since it was preferable to be wet than shot, the soldiers dug willy-nilly, and suffered in consequence until drainage, pumps, revetments to hold the soil and similar measures were gradually brought into play.

Probably the highest level reached in this specialised form of fortification engineering was that of the German Army in their construction of the 'Siegfried Stellung', more often known by its English name 'The Hindenburg Line'. This was begun in September 1916 as a strong defensive position, at that time well to the rear of the German front line, extending from the Belgian coast to

Pont-à-Musson on the Moselle, the object being to prepare at relative leisure for occupation at a future date when the Army would be withdrawn from its extended line.

The plan was to emplace forward look-outs in twos and threes some 500 metres in advance of the main line of resistance; this line would be established on a reverse slope so as to give greater concealment and protection from Allied fire. Between the outpost line and the main line was a scattering of pickets intended to hold up an enemy advance. Behind the main line were concrete blockhouses commanding the entire zone with interlocking fields of fire. Then came a second line of trench, of exceptional width in order to be impassable to tanks, behind which lay the second manned trench line strongly held with troops available for counter-attacking should the front line fall. Within each line the trenches were carefully built, with armour-plated loopholes for riflemen and machine gunners, ample drainage, liberally supplied with gas-proof and bomb-proof concrete underground shelters in which the troops could live in moderate comfort. Once this forward zone was completed a third rear zone was built on similar lines, and in

some areas a fourth, so that eventually the defensive zone was three to four miles deep, a continuous belt of entrenchments, blockhouses, tunnels, and the most dense and impenetrable belts of barbed wire ever erected.

The entire line was ninety miles long and was intended to be manned by twenty divisions. The original programme called for completion of the first two lines in five months, and 50,000 Russian prisoners-of-war were used for labouring, plus 3000 Belgians and 12,000 German soldiers and civilian workmen. Light railways were laid to bring up the immense quantities of cement, steel, wire and other supplies.

The disengagement of the German Army and its withdrawal to the Siegfried Stellung in March 1917 was one of the most skilful strategic manoeuvres ever performed in war, thirty-five divisions being moved back in good order and leaving nothing but wasteland behind them. The relocation shortened the German line by some twenty miles, provided thirteen divisions for reserve, and put the front-line soldiers into vastly stronger and more comfortable positions than they had previously occupied. It was to be a year before the Allies were able to make any impression on the new line.

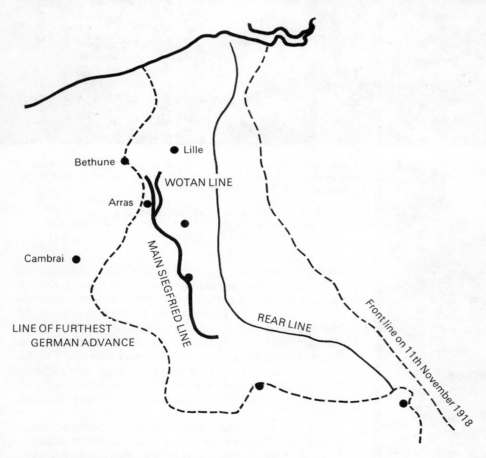

The Siegfried Line, showing the main and rear lines, together with the battle lines of 1918

Chapter Seven

The Ferro-Concrete Revival

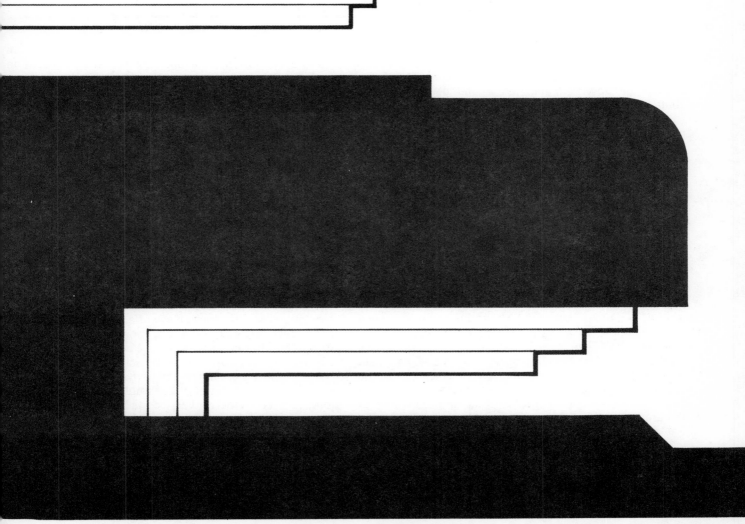

Turret Outline

Turret Shaft

Magazine

Fire Control and
Computing Room

Hydraulic Tanks,
Accumulator and
Air Compressor
Room

Engine Room

Store

To Entrance

Plan of the Japanese 30.5-cm. coast
gun turret at Uraga, Tokyo Bay.

Section of the Uraga turret.

After the First World War had ended it looked, to many observers, as if the royal and ancient art of fortification had been completely and finally discredited. The Krupp and Skoda howitzers had left a trail of ruined forts, shattered masonry and uprooted cupolas from Belgium to the Urals. The remains were swept away, or left to moulder, or, as with Douaumont, tidied up and kept as commemorative monuments to the men who had died defending them. But in general the armies of the world turned their backs on masonry and armour; Britain and the U.S.A. disposed of most of their coast defence forts, relying henceforth on open batteries, while the frontiers of Europe were, for the first time in centuries, no longer watched by caponiers and redoubts.

Strangely, the only postwar move towards armoured defences was in Japan who, only five years previously, had demonstrated the relative futility of permanent fortification such as Tsingtao. Entirely unknown to the West — and, indeed, unknown there until relatively recently — a move began in 1919 to bring the Japanese coast defences to a high pitch of efficiency. In 1918 a decision had been taken to earmark an area near Saeki, on the Bundo Strait leading to the Inland Sea, as a fleet anchorage and base. As befitted a martial island race the Japanese had always set considerable store by coast defence artillery, and in order to command the waters of the area, and also to deny entrance to the strait, a new artillery installation was designed. Whether the inspira-

tion came from the American work at Fort Drum we shall never know, but the fact remains that the installation took the form of a converted naval turret mounting two 30.5-cm. guns with a range of 32,200 yards. Very little is known of this installation; it was operational by 1920, but apparently during a target practice firing in 1923 there was an explosion which killed all the turret crew and wrecked the installation beyond repair. The turret remains were dismantled, though the concrete magazine and other ancillaries remain there today, with a monument in front to commemorate the victims of the accident, and the defence of the area was thereafter reliant upon a number of smaller guns, and a controlled submarine minefield across the entrance to the strait.

However, this unfortunate accident had not altered the Japanese Army's opinions on the value of turret installations, and a programme of modernisation of their defences was planned. Then, in 1923, as a result of the decisions of the Washington Conference on Naval Limitations, the Japanese Navy offered a number of guns and turrets, originally intended for new battleships, to the Army. The offer comprised three 41-cm., six 30-cm., two 25-cm. and two 20-cm. turrets, each mounting two guns. A more or less standardised pattern of work was developed. The 41-cm. turret, for example, was some 40 feet long, 30 feet wide and 9 feet tall above the ground, constructed of 12-in. armour on the sides and face and 4-in. armour on the roof. A concrete and steel lined shaft in the ground supported the turret structure, which extended some 30 feet down, the whole revolving mass being carried on a tapered roller race about 8 feet below ground level. No armoured glacis was used to protect the lower edge of the turret, the engineers rightly assuming the virtual impossibility of hitting such a tiny target by gunfire from a ship. Below ground there was a tunnel complex containing magazines, accommodation, power house and other ancillaries, together with a forced draught ventilation plant which prevented fumes or smoke from the gun from entering the turret when firing.

The small turrets were on much the same plan though, doubtless due to their shorter range, they were ingeniously camouflaged by laying 6 inches of concrete on the turret roof, covering that with a foot of earth, and sowing the earth with grass and weeds to match the surrounding vegetation. Trenches dug in the ground in front of the turrets allowed the barrels to be depressed into them and covered with camouflage netting to prevent aerial detection. No such measures appear to have been taken with the 41-cm. and 30-cm. turrets; possibly it was felt that their construction was so solid that attack did not matter, and camouflage was confined to painting.

The turrets were ingeniously sited to best advantage. On the south coast of Korea, near Pusan, was a 41-cm. turret; on the Island of Tsushima another, with two 30-cm. turrets; and on the Island of Iki Shima a third 41-cm. turret and one 30-cm. turret, all so sited that their arcs of fire interlocked and completely closed the waters between Japan and Korea. Of the remaining turrets, one 30-cm. turret went to Tsuguru to cover the strait between the islands of Hokkaidu and Honshu and the four smaller turrets were disposed around Tokyo Bay. An interesting tactical feature of their disposition is that in many cases there was no attempt to obtain the greatest possible arc of fire by siting them in relatively exposed positions; if such arcs were obtainable, well and good, but the concealment of the turret seems to have been the primary consideration. Certainly in at least one application – a turret at Sunosaki, at the southwest entrance to Tokyo Bay – the turret had an arc of fire which could not bear on hostile vessels until they were actually in the Bay and stern-on to the guns, travelling away from them. There may have been sound reasons for siting guns in this way, but apart from any other considerations, it argues a great deal of confidence in the fire control, range-finding and gunnery abilities of the battery.

Apart from this activity, and the addition of coastal defences to various Pacific Islands by the Japanese, there was virtually no work done on any kind of fortification throughout the 1920s. Then, in the early 1930s, came the inspiration of M. Maginot.

Maginot was a member of the Chamber of Deputies of France; he had survived the war after experiencing its horrors at first hand as a sergeant of infantry, and he, together with most of his contemporaries, was determined that the affair should not happen again. He therefore proposed a line of defensive works following the French frontier from the Channel to the Swiss border; not merely a collection of detached forts, but a continuous sub-

M. Andre Maginot, 1877–1932. *Radio Times Hulton Picture Library.*

terranean position whose only outward and visible sign would be retractable steel turrets carrying artillery, smaller cupolas with machine guns, breech-loading mortars and anti-tank guns, and observation cupolas. What Maginot's proposal boiled down to, in fact, was simply the trench line of 1914–18, prepared in advance and with every conceivable refinement. If trench warfare was to be the pattern of war in the future, then France would be prepared for it, with the last possible word in trenches built and manned (with 300,000 men) before the first shot was fired. It was to be the Siegfried Stellung, but built in peace-time.

Beneath the ground would be barracks linked by electric underground railways, power stations, artesian wells, everything necessary to life and defence. Since the whole was to be connected, reinforcements and supplies of food and ammunition could be rapidly shifted along the railway system from convenient depots to any particular sector under attack. Since the turrets would be in such profusion that the fields of fire would interlock, it would be impossible for any enemy to pass the line, and because of the subterranean lines of supply a siege would be impossible. Mines would be out of the question since the works would be far too deep to be attacked in such a manner, and, in any case, sensitive

A gun turret in the Maginot Line. A 75-mm. gun is being loaded in the background, while members of the detachment are setting fuzes on shrapnel shells in the foreground. *Imperial War Museum.*

microphones buried in the earth would soon detect such attempts and the provision of countermine galleries would enable them to be dealt with.

We need not involve ourselves with the political arguments which followed on the heels of this proposal; suffice it to say that within a surprisingly short time — for such was the anti-war attitude of the day — the proposals were accepted, money was allotted and work began. It seems incredible when one remembers the German outflanking move in August 1914, but the plan for the Maginot Line was modified by bringing it to a halt at Montmédy, near the junction of the French and Belgian/German borders; this, it is said, was in order to avoid offending the Belgians, which must qualify as one of history's weakest excuses.

The effort thrown into the Maginot Line was immense, millions of francs being voted to its construction, and the result can only be described as luxurious in comparison with any fortification previously built. Once a large proportion of it had been built, the propaganda films and stories lost little in the telling of the magnificence and impenetrability of the structure, and this took effect in various quarters in various ways. In France it doubtless inspired the populace with a feeling of security against the rising tide of National Socialist Germany on the far side, and it is tempting to speculate how much it contributed to the malaise which manifested itself in 1940.

In Germany in the early 1930s the reaction was what might have been expected; in 1935 the War Office telephoned Krupp's and asked about how powerful a gun would have to be in order to penetrate the assumed thickness of the Maginot Line. Krupp's replied by calculating ballistic data for three hypothetical weapons of 70-cm. (27.5 in.), 80-cm. (31.5 in.) and 100-cm. (39.4 in.) calibre. In March 1936 Adolf Hitler visited the Krupp Works and in the course of his tour asked more or less the same question. As a result, Krupp's began designing a monster 80-cm. calibre railway gun to fire a 6.98-ton concrete-piercing shell. Early in 1937 the drawings were

In opposition to the Maginot Line, the Germans constructed their second Siegfried Line. These 15-cm. turret guns formed part of this defence of the Western frontier of Germany. *Imperial War Museum.*

Map of the Maginot Line. Guderian's panzers drove through the unprotected Ardennes sector.

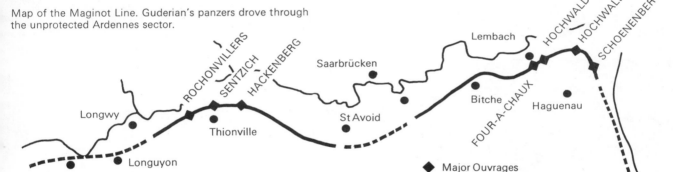

shown to the Army, approved, and in the summer of that year manufacture of the weapon began, with a promise of delivery by the spring of 1940.

In Switzerland the construction of the Maginot Line was followed with some interest, and plans were drawn up for the construction of deep bomb-proof structures to house arsenals, food stores, even factories, and work on this project was put in hand in about 1937, though under conditions of much greater secrecy than obtained with work on the Maginot Line. Although not directly concerned with the mounting of ordnance or the repelling of attack, the constructional techniques of the fortress engineer were called upon in order to obtain adequate protection in these works, and shortly after it had begun the plans were expanded to begin a series of underground defensive works as well, to reinforce the natural defences of the Alpine passes. Armoured turrets made their appearance once more but, like the Maginot Line, the major portion of the redoubts were well beneath the ground, and not, as in Brialmont's works, above the surface and covered with a relatively thin layer of earth.

The Belgians too, decided to bring their defences back into service, and new works, modifications of Brialmont to all intents and purposes, made their appearance on the German frontier, while Poland endeavoured to consolidate her hard-won frontiers by construction of a variety of concrete works on the German and Russian borders and the building of a modern coast defence fortress on the Hel Peninsula. By 1937 construction was in full swing all over Europe, and the concrete mixers were working overtime.

When the storm broke in 1939 the French Army immediately shut themselves into the Maginot Line and prepared for the onslaught. The German Panzer divisions tore into Poland, bypassing the forts and leaving them to wither, though the bitter fight on the Hel peninsula

Opposite above: As Europe armed, so did America; one of the first between-wars installations was this 16-in. gun guarding the Panama Canal. Notice the complete absence of any form of fortification, protection relying solely upon siting behind a crest. Notice too the complete failure to provide against attack from the air. Below: subsequent American 16-in. installations were in concrete casemated works of sufficient strength to resist aerial bombing.

which, being a peninsula, had to be taken the hard way, has entered Polish legend. It was not until 1940 that fortifications played much part in the war.

On 8th April 1940 the German forces attacked Norway, and at 11.15 pm that night a patrol vessel in the Outer Oslo Fjord reported the approach of a number of unknown warships: it opened fire, hit one, and was almost immediately destroyed by overwhelming fire. Due to a sea fog, the fortresses in the vicinity could not bring effective fire to bear, but by 00.30 hours on the 9th the approaching fleet had been identified as German. It consisted of, among other vessels, the pocket-battleship *Lutzow*, the cruisers *Emden* and *Blücher*, and the gunnery training ship *Brummer*.

On receiving the early reports, the forts at Oskarsborg, further up the fjord, were manned, and at 03.30 the look-outs saw the first ship approaching. A 28-cm. gun battery opened fire and the first two shells struck the *Blücher*, on the fire turret and abaft the bridge, wrecking the fire control centre. A 15-cm battery also opened fire, demolishing the *Blücher*'s bridge with high explosive shells. The 28-cm. battery kept up a fire with 28-cm. armour-piercing shells against the waterline, and within a short time flames and smoke poured from the vessel and its speed had dropped to about 5 knots. As the ship passed the 28-cm. battery, it came within range of a land-based torpedo installation which fired two torpedoes, one of which struck the *Blücher*'s engine room and the other the ship's torpedo magazine. With an enormous explosion the vessel stopped and began to list; the crew began to leap overboard, and the ship slowly turned on its side and sank.

The fortress guns now turned on the *Brummer* and severely damaged it, and the invasion fleet turned about and sailed back out of range. Early next morning an estimated fifty aircraft appeared over the forts and began a bombing attack which lasted almost all day, relays of bombers coming in to take over the attack. During the day too, the *Lutzow* shelled the works at a range of 11,000 metres from time to time. The guns were in open barbette positions, protected by earth and concrete parapets and armoured shields, while the detachments were provided with strong bomb-proof shelters. In spite of an estimated 500 bombs and 100 shells, no gun was damaged. In the end the German fleet landed its troops south of the batteries and made an outflanking move to take Oslo, after which the coast batteries were attacked from the land side. They finally surrendered only when Norway fell.

This small and relatively little-known action of the batteries on Kalholmen Island had an effect out of all proportion to its magnitude. The German invasion fleet,

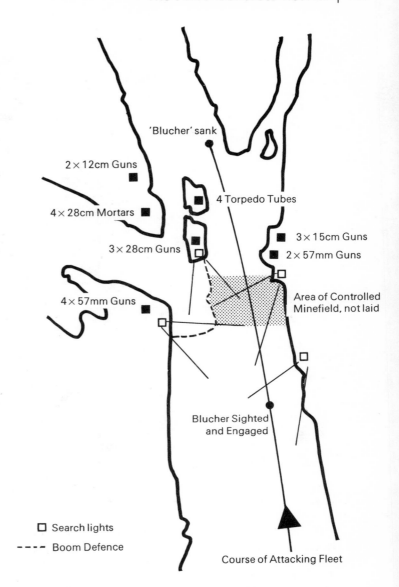

Map of Oslo Fiord, showing Oskarsborg Fortress and the course of the German fleet in its attempt to run past.

supremely confident, was quite sure it could sail straight into Oslo and, by sheer surprise, take the town. But the action fought by the fortress and its effect on the German fleet imposed a delay on the invaders' programme, allowing the King of Norway and his Government to escape from Oslo and the bullion of the Bank of Norway to be removed to safety. Moreover it was later found that the *Blücher* had been carrying a number of administrative officials and secret police, intended to take over the administration of the conquered country; most of these key men drowned when the ship was sunk, and their loss was an additional setback to German plans. Similar actions, it must be said, were fought by other Norwegian batteries; at one fort, Agdenes on Trondheim Fjord, twenty-five gunners kept a 500-man German landing force held up for the better part of a day before they were finally subdued.

German pioneer troops using flame-throwers and shaped charges against a cupola in the Fort of Eben Emael in 1940.

But by the time the news of these actions came out of Norway, the eyes of the world were once more directed to France and Flanders. The Germans had at last exploded the 'Sitzkrieg' or 'Phoney War' and moved against France; and, as in 1914, they moved through Belgium, outflanking the carefully prepared Maginot Line. The planned advance included a line between Liège and Maastricht, a gap which was efficiently covered by the fort of Eben Emael, a new work built during the 1930s and one which appeared to be impregnable. The lessons of Liège had not been entirely wasted on the Belgian engineers and they had, while adhering to Brialmont's basic layout, made the work immensely strong, of best quality concrete and with armoured turrets. As well as being ditched, it was effectively guarded by the Albert Canal on the German side, and a conventional attack was obviously going to be a costly, if not impossible, operation. Moreover the German Army had no super-heavy artillery it could call upon to repeat the feats of 1914; only one of the 42-cm. Krupp weapons, a 'Gamma' howitzer, survived, and it was securely anchored in concrete in a proving ground. The promised 80-cm. railway gun was still being made, the construction having been delayed by a number of technical problems, so there was no help to be looked for in that direction.

But this didn't matter at all; the technique which was to subdue Eben Emael had been planned in advance, and it introduced a new dimension into warfare; it is reputed to have been proposed by Hitler himself, though there is no confirmation of this. Instead of a massive army appearing at the gate and laying siege to it, Eben Emael was to be attacked by rather more than a hundred men who were to be landed immediately on top of the work, literally on the roof of the redoubt and well inside the various obstacles, by glider.

The airborne force duly landed and roamed at will about the outside of the work, shooting into embrasures and loopholes, but they had little prospect of getting much further without heavier assistance for blowing in doors and wrecking cupolas. This was provided, in a manner highly reminiscent of Douaumont, by another pioneer sergeant, this time named Steffen, leading another pioneer platoon. While the airborne assault on the roof kept the occupants busy, Steffen and his men crossed the

The massive German 80-cm. railway gun 'Gustav'; originally intended as a means of breaking through the Maginot Line, it was not finished in time. It later took part in the Siege of Sevastopol in 1942, where this picture was taken. *Imperial War Museum.*

A typical anti-concrete shell, this one being for the Russian 152-mm. gun M1937.

Albert Canal in inflatable boats, taking with them heavy demolition charges, flame-throwers, 'Bangalore torpedoes' for wire-cutting, and a number of the then-revolutionary 'hollow charge demolition mines'. Cutting and blasting their way through the wire and other obstacles surrounding the redoubt, Steffen's platoon joined the airborne infantry and set about prising open the fort.

Flame-throwers directed at the gun ports in the turrets effectively put an end to any resistance from the occupants, while charges of TNT at the turret edges and on the gun barrels jammed the turrets and ruined the guns. The hollow charge units, placed on top of the turrets, blew holes straight through the armour, and the jet of flame and molten metal passed into the turret structure, completely wrecking the internal machinery. Hollow charges and demolition charges were then used against doors, ventilators, periscopes, every item which could conceivably be attacked, and in a very short time the pioneers had opened the fort to allow the airborne troops to enter and round up the surviving occupants. With no artillery, indeed with nothing heavier than could be conveniently carried by one man, one of the strongest and most formidable forts in Europe had been reduced to impotence in a couple of hours.

In spite of this spectacular feat of arms, and in spite of the Maginot Line being by-passed, the German Army still pursued its search for a perfected artillery system for dealing with hard targets. The technique used against Eben Emael was exceptional, would not suit all cases, and, moreover, was one of those tricks of war which once used are easily countered when repeated – a few

Parts of the Maginot Line held out in 1940 and these German photographs depict the assault on a position near Ste Menhoud, using flame and satchel charges

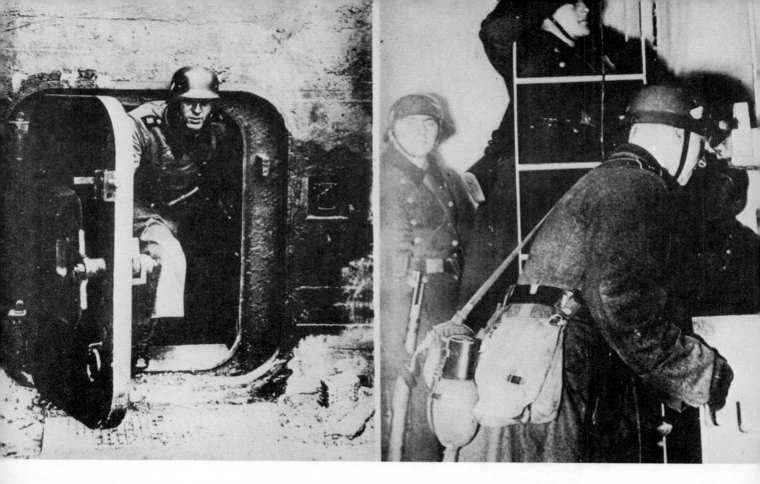

Above: The Siegfried Line; one of the armoured entrance doors and the interior of a defence post. *Imperial War Museum.*

Below: One of the many belts of concrete tank obstacles forming part of the Siegfried Line defences and taking the place of the earlier Abattis. *Imperial War Museum.*

anti-aircraft guns and machine guns on top of the redoubt would soon put a stop to any attempt to repeat that particular manoeuvre. As it happened Röchling Eisen und Stahlwerk of Düsseldorf had been drawn to the question of defeating concrete and steel by artillery fire, and they had begun by making a fundamental reassessment of what the problem involved and what were the contemporary views on it.

The standard anti-concrete shell of the day was a projectile with a simple conical head, made of steel having about 45 tons to the square inch yield strength, and with a relatively small content of high explosive initiated by a base fuze. In order to promote efficiency in flight, the conical nose was covered by a tapering steel ballistic cap or windshield. In essence, it was a de-rated armour-piercing shell, differing principally in the shape of its nose and by having slightly more explosive inside. The principles and formula on which these shells were designed had not changed since the days when Becker designed the 42-cm. shells for Krupp in 1912, and Röchling's now took a fresh look at the matter. The basic premise was very simple; one concentrated as much energy into the tip of the shell as could be attained, and the simple rule of thumb was that penetration would improve in proportion to the ratio W/D^3, W being the weight of the shell and D its diameter.

But so long as the projectile was a spun shell fired from a rifled gun in the conventional fashion, there was a limit to the weight of shell; this was due to the fact that the diameter was unalterably fixed by the size of the gun and the length restricted to not much more than five

Field Marshal Rommel inspecting a concrete casemate, part of the German 'Atlantic Wall' defences. *Imperial War Museum.*

times the calibre, since shells of greater length than this were almost impossible to stabilize by spinning and hence became unstable in flight and inaccurate.

Röchling resolved this dilemma by designing a very long shell and stabilising it in flight by putting fins on its rear end. Developed for the standard 21-cm. howitzer, the shell was 17-cm. in calibre, and it was supported at its head by a 'sabot' or sleeve of 21-cm. calibre, while a similar sleeve supported the base end and also kept the flexible fins wrapped around the shell base. When fired the two sabots were flung clear of the shell as it emerged from the gun muzzle, the fins sprang out into the airstream and the shell flew accurately to its target. It was 102 inches long — 15.25 times its calibre — and weighed 425 lbs, so that on reaching the target it delivered a blow of about 9600 foot-tons, or about 455 tons per inch area of shell. The efficiency of this can be gauged from the figures on the 42-cm. shell used in 1914; though heavier, they were over twice the calibre of the Röchling shell and developed only 350 tons per inch of area.

Certainly the performance lived up to Röchling's expectations. As a trial, a number were fired against a captured fort near Neufchateau in Belgium; the shells

(devoid of explosive for the purpose of the trial) penetrated 3 metres of earth cover, 3.6 metres of concrete, a layer of masonry, passed through a storeroom, through the stone floor and came to rest 5 metres below in the earth. When filled with explosive the shells were fuzed so that when retardation stopped — as when the shell broke through the cover into a gallery or casemate — the explosive was detonated.

Some 8000 of these shells were made and stockpiled, but they saw very little use. It is believed that a handful were fired against the fortress of Brest-Litovsk when the Germans advanced against Russia in 1941, though there are no records of the results achieved. After this, Hitler, having been apprised of the performance of the Röchling shell, forbade their use without his personal authorisation, fearing that in the case of an undamaged specimen being captured, the design might be copied and used against German defences. Since commanders were reluctant to seek permission, the shells gradually got forgotten and were never used.

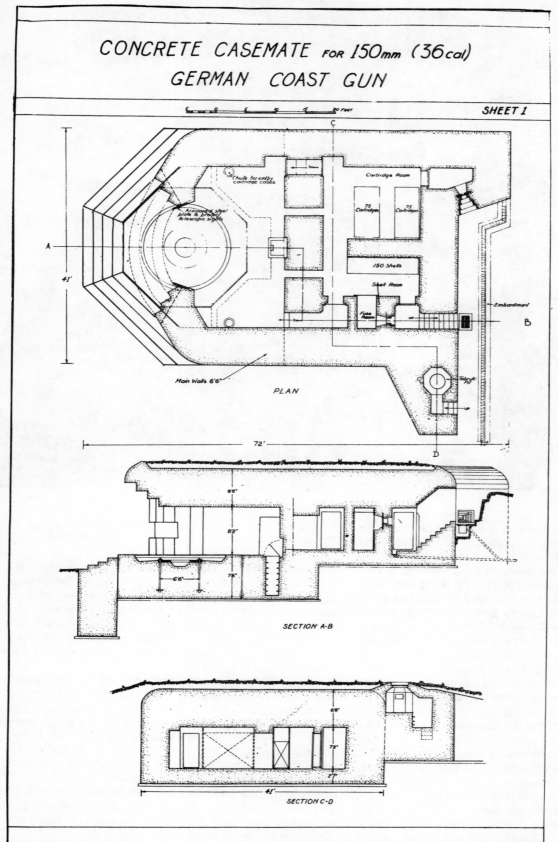

CONCRETE CASEMATE FOR 150mm (36cal) GERMAN COAST GUN

SHEET 1

20 FEET

PLAN

Chute for empty cartridge cases

Armoured steel plate to protect telescopic sights

Cartridge Room

75 Cartridges

75 Cartridges

150 Shells

Shell Room

Fuse Room

Embankment

Tobruk Pit

Main Walls 6'6"

41'

72'

SECTION A-B

6'8"

8'2"

7'6"

6'6"

SECTION C-D

6'8"

7'2"

41'

A Martian report. Plan of a German 15-cm. gun casemate of the same pattern as that shown in the photograph on the previous page. Notice the armoured throat to the gun port, the 'Tobruk Pit' for a local defence machine-gun, and the machine-gun port facing down the entrance passage.

Hitler's apprehensive fear was, of course, largely conditioned by the fact that the 'Organisation Todt' were busy erecting enormous quantities of fortifications on the borders of Germany and on the North Sea Coast in order to defend 'Festung Europa' against Allied invasion. The Todt organisation was a massive civil engineering complex which existed solely to provide a construction corps for the armed forces of the Reich: it was para-military in structure and operation, and was certainly one of the most efficient organs of the German war machine. But the fortifications they produced were notable more for their bulk and profusion than for their artifice; the day of the fortress engineer laying out a trace, ditching, adding bastions, lunettes and ravelins, bomb-proofs and caponiers, was over. Fire-power now replaced obstacles; the German Machine Gun 42 (MG 42) could fire at 1200 rounds a minute, and the presence of a couple of those was more of an obstacle than any ravelin or counterguard.

As a result the defensive posts of the Todt designs were little more than monolithic concrete blocks, pierced by gun ports and containing sufficient internal compartmentation to house whatever force was needed. The only link with the past appears to have been the practice of dog-legging the entrance and covering it with a port through which a machine gun could fire. The exterior angles were generally rounded in an attempt to deflect projectiles and the works were, where possible, sunk into a forward slope to give some degree of flank protection. Where this was not possible, then they were sited where they were needed and then camouflaged as best as could be managed; sometimes even this was impossible, and the erection stood out from its surroundings like a flagpole; at other times the camouflage was so ingenious as to defy discovery.

British Intelligence agencies spent the years from the occupation of France to the invasion in collecting, by means of aerial photographs, agents and little-publicised raids, every scrap of information they could gain about the defences of the 'Atlantic Wall', issuing periodic 'Martian Reports'. graded Top Secret, and listing all the designs and locations as they were discovered. By mid-1944 they had tabulated no less than 675 separate and distinct designs of pill-box, casemate, observation post and gun mounting, ranging from simple squares of concrete to involved structures with armoured cupolas for observation and armoured roofs over the guns. The most spectacular were the enormous casemated gun batteries

at Noires Mottes (near Sangatte) mounting the three 40.6-cm. ex-Naval guns of Batterie Lindemann, and those containing four 30.5-cm. guns of Batterie Friedrich August at Wimereaux. These gigantic structures were impossible to camouflage and simply relied on massive thickness — up to 10 metres — of reinforced concrete to render them immune to any conceivable form of attack.

As well as concrete works, new ideas in obstacles also made an appearance; complex structures of steel laid out to sea in such a fashion as to deny access to the shore or deny entrance to rivers, lying just below the surface at high tide to foul the bottom of any craft attempting to come close. Not only did they rely on their intrinsic destructiveness, they were also liberally laced with a variety of mines and explosive devices intended to both damage craft which struck the obstacle and also to deter any attempts at removal.

Somehow or other the Allied armies had to overcome this array of defensive works, and the particular difficulty lay in that it was largely at the edge of the English Channel or the Atlantic Ocean. The ditch for this fortress

was of a vast width, and no amount of sapping and paralleling on the other side of it was going to do any good. The besiegers had to cross the ditch, throw themselves at the escarp wall and hope for the best. As a result of this appraisal, the hunt began for weapons which would defeat this colossal acreage of concrete. At the same time the planners cast round for some line of approach which would avoid a head-on collision with the worst of the new defences, since with all the Organisation Todt's expertise and manpower it was impossible for them to construct a rampart stretching from the Pyrenees to the Skagerrak, and construction had been concentrated into the areas which were, in the opinion of the German Army, most liable to attack.

It is frequently believed that during the Second World War the only people who produced 'secret weapons' were the Germans; this is far from true. The Allied side produced quite a lot, though since many of them were never used they were little known and less mentioned. Moreover quite a number of them survived to be post-war secret weapons. But some of the weapons developed

Left: One of the massive emplacements for the 40-cm. guns of Batterie Lindemann, near Calais. *Imperial War Museum.*

Opposite page: One of the many varieties of steel obstacle strewn across the French beaches to deter invaders. *Robert Hunt Library.*

Above: The 'Wallbuster' shell; the plastic explosive was contained in the wire mesh bag which pancaked against the target on impact. *Ian Hogg.*

were a direct result of the hard thinking which had been going on about the problems of breaking into the Fortress of Europe. One of the most prolific designers was Sir Dennis Burney, a highly talented engineer in many fields. He had been concerned with airship design in the 1920s and 1930s, among other things, and early in the war he began experimenting with a recoilless gun. Without delving too deeply into the ballistics of the thing, its action can be explained relatively simply by saying that a proportion of the gas generated by the exploding cartridge was directed to the rear of the gun through one or more nozzles, the remaining gas driving the shell out of the gun in the usual way. Thus there was a jet reaction to force the weapon forward, and by careful design this would exactly balance the rearward recoil of the gun. The German Army, it should be added, also came up with the same idea; but the Burney gun was taken a step further. Due to the peculiar ballistics, Sir Dennis was able to produce a gun with a light barrel, and following from this he reasoned that he should be able to make a shell with a lightweight body and a much greater capacity

for explosive than had ever been managed before; this was due to the low acceleration within the gun barrel which put less strain on the shell during firing.

With this as a starting point he developed a thin-walled shell containing a large quantity of plastic explosive; when the shell struck a hard target, the thin wall collapsed and the plastic explosive spread on to the target like a poultice, there to be detonated by a fuze in the base of the shell. The result was to drive a detonation wave at extremely high velocity into the wall, which it traversed due to the homogeneity of the material until it came to the rear face. There, for a variety of reasons, among them one called the 'Hopkinson Pressure-Bar Effect', the wave bounced back, but in doing so it overstressed the rear face and caused a section of it to be detached and flung off at high speed.

Sir Dennis now made a 7.2-in. recoilless gun and produced a design of 'Wallbuster' shell for it; on 29th October 1943 it was given its first trial against a 5-feet thick reinforced concrete wall, and astonished everybody by blowing the rear face of the wall in pieces some 60

Lightweight firepower; the British 3.45-in. recoilless gun being fired from a man's shoulder. *Ian Hogg.*

Close-up of the recoiling Spigot Mortar on an AVRE tank. At the right is a 40-lb 'Flying Dustbin' demolition bomb. *Imperial War Museum.*

feet away and cutting all the internal reinforcing rods. Even if the projectile had failed to penetrate, it was obvious that any defender behind the wall, or any weapon, would have felt hard done by and would have been in no condition to put up any sort of resistance to attack. A further advantage of the Burney gun was that being recoilless it could be fired from a landing craft without unduly straining the vessel — provided some precautions were taken over the back blast — and the entire gun only weighed 32 hundredweight, instead of the $14\frac{1}{2}$ tons of the service 7.2-in. howitzer of conventional pattern. Production of a number of recoilless guns to arm the leading elements of the invasion force was authorised.

There were other people looking at the same problem; in August 1943 a report on 'Rocket Projectiles for the Attack of Reinforced Concrete Walls and Pillboxes' was prepared by the experimental rocket establishment at Aberporth in Cardiganshire, and after discussions by various interested parties work began on a rocket-propelled piercing shell, later called 'Lilo'. It was little

Another old siege technique was revived for the assault on France; the Escalade. Here is a 100-foot Merryweather Fire Escape on a truck, intended for scaling cliffs. *Ian Hogg.*

Below: The escalading ladder erected; when prepared for the invasion the head of the ladder was fitted with steel armoured shields and twin machine guns. Other versions of this ladder were fitted to amphibious vehicles. *Ian Hogg.*

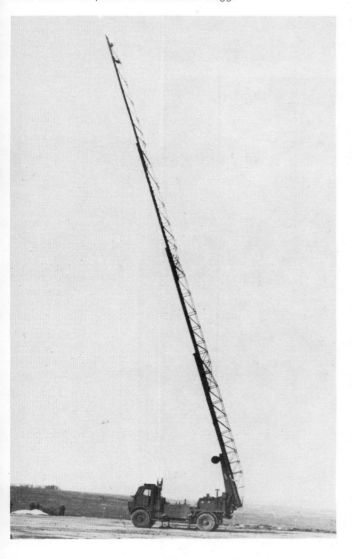

more than a conventional steel shell hung on the front of a 3-in. anti-aircraft rocket motor, but it had the advantage that it could be carried, emplaced and fired by one man. In the event it was never used in Europe but it proved to be a formidable device for dealing with palm-tree bunkers in the Pacific theatre of war.

Another interested group were the 79th Armoured Division who, under the direction of Major-General P. C. S. Hobart, were hard at work developing a variety of specialised tanks, which were collectively known throughout the Army as 'The Funnies'. One of these odd vehicles was the Armoured Vehicle, Royal Engineers or 'AVRE', which was intended to deliver a massive demolition charge at short range. This had the advantage that the tank protected the operators from any ill effects due to the proximity of the weapon's effect; it was probably this liability to be too close for comfort which led to the weapon being code-named 'Petard'. The troops preferred to call it the 'Flying Dustbin' from the size of the projectiles, while the official name, less inspiring, was the 'Mortar, Recoiling Spigot'. No matter what it was called it hurled a 40-lb bomb for about a hundred yards; trials showed that a reinforced concrete wall 6 feet thick could be breached by eight or nine shots, and a further trial demonstrated the ability of the weapon to blow a sufficient hole in a wall 10 feet thick to allow the Churchill tank (on which the device was mounted) to drive through. Since the Petard was a much more simple, not to say primitive, weapon than the recoilless gun, the production of the gun was abandoned in favour of the Petard.

Some of the ideas put forward were on what might, without malice, be called the lunatic fringe of ballistics; there was, for example, a 10.5-in. recoilless gun called 'Ardeer Aggie' which obtained recoillessness by launching its projectile forward while at the same time launching an equal weight of sandbags rearward. At one stage there was a proposal to mount this on a tank, but the prospects of a few hundred pounds of sandbag being propelled into the ranks of the supporting troops was sufficient to dissuade even its most fervent supporters.

Another idea was to add a rocket motor to the warhead of the Petard bomb, mount a number of these missiles outside the tank body and fire them in one salvo to start the wall-breaching operation. This was turned down on the grounds of the risk to the tank and its occupants from driving into battle festooned with high explosive. 'Conkernut' was next suggested, a wall-buster head of 37 lbs of plastic explosive fired by rocket from an aircraft; while this worked well enough, it was of itself insufficient to breach a wall, and the accuracy of fire necessary to obtain a succession of hits on the same section of wall could not be guaranteed. Finally, mention must be made of the 'Great Panjandrum', a pair of wheels ten feet in diameter, rocket driven, carrying a demolition charge at the wheel's hub. The idea was that the rockets, tangentially mounted on the wheel rims, would propel the affair up a beach until it struck a defensive wall or pill-box, there to detonate. A vast amount of time and energy was wasted on this firework, every trial ending in disaster

The 'Scissors' bridging
tank, demonstrating its
ability to span a ditch.
Imperial War Museum.

A flame-throwing tank
demonstrating its ability
to fry anything in its path.

A French coast defence gun in a casemate at Cherbourg

more spectacular than the previous trial, and eventually it too was abandoned.

In the end, of course, the time came to put all these ideas and tactics to the test. The planners had selected as the objective an area less formidably fortified than most areas and the invasion moved in. As well as the simple matter of breaching walls and works, there were problems anticipated in such mundane areas as scaling seawalls which were as steep and well defended as any escarp wall had ever been; the obstacles had to be neutralised, the minefields breached, and finally the defenders dealt with. To supplement all these things a variety of mechanical contrivances appeared: tanks bearing bundles of wood paling to be dropped into ditches; tanks carrying roadways on their upper surface, which could be driven against a wall to act as escalading ramps or into ditches to form expendable bridges; tanks with girder bridges to cross wider ditches; tanks with flame-throwers, tanks with petards, and just-plain-tanks which poured fire into the defences to keep the defenders' heads down while the specialist machines lumbered forward and performed their manifold tricks. Coupled with bombing

from the air and bombardment from the sea, the Atlantic Wall was breached in a matter of hours, and the discrediting of fortification was complete.

Certain works remained, however, against which a weapon was developed that put Big Bertha and the Röchling Shell into the background. These works, while perhaps not fortification in the correct sense, were far more massive than anything previously built, and they certainly had to be considered as fortifications when it came to discussing methods of attacking them. These were the massive U-Boat 'pens' built at various of the Atlantic ports: Brest, Lorient, St Nazaire, Narvik and others. These huge covered docks were of immense thickness — anything from 18 to 25 feet of reinforced concrete of the finest quality. Normal bombs made no impression; even the 12,000-lb 'Block-buster' did little more than remove a few feet of the surface, and a near miss, lethal to any other building, made not the slightest impression on these structures. The problem had been

seen by the Royal Air Force towards the end of 1943 when they had asked the Ordnance Board 'to consider a bomb of about 4000 lbs weight, capable of penetrating 20 feet of concrete when dropped from a height of 20,000 feet.' Already, in fact, work had begun on a weapon which would produce the answer, but it had begun in the Royal Navy: a 4500-lb piercing bomb propelled by an aggregate of nineteen 3-in. rocket motors attached to its rear end. The story of how this bomb was devised, and the political 'in-fighting' which went on in getting it adopted (it was resisted by the RAF, apparently on account of its high NIH factor) (NIH = Not Invented Here) is a long and interesting story which has been excellently told elsewhere by the man who invented it (*Admiralty Brief* by Edward Terrel) but at last the Rocket Bomb entered service and surpassed even the most optimistic expectation. As well as U-Boat pens, the bombs were used to attack rocket launching structures

Above: A German submarine under repair in the safety of a U-boat pen at St Nazaire. *Imperial War Museum.*

Above right: The exterior of the pens at St Nazaire, illustrating the massive thickness of the roofs. *Imperial War Museum.*

Below right: A RAF Lancaster releases a 22,000 lb 'Grand Slam' bomb. *Imperial War Museum.*

of similar immensity, and at one of these, examined shortly after the area had been liberated by the invasion troops, one bomb was discovered to have penetrated 20 feet of reinforced concrete and then detonated, displacing about 350 tons of concrete.

At about the same time as the U-Boat pens were being attacked, an interesting and unusual affair was being concluded in the Far East; the U.S. Army were about to re-take the Manila Forts. In 1941 the Japanese had attacked the United States, and in 1942 the Americans

A selection of bombs, from 40 to 22,000 lbs in weight. Only The 'Tallboy' and 'Grand Slam' were of much use against fortifications, and then only by virtue of their 'earthquake' effect; their penetrative ability was relatively small. *Imperial War Museum.*

were forced to surrender the fortress of Corregidor and its companion works, including the 'Concrete Battleship', Fort Drum. Before surrendering the guns were spiked by removing the breech-blocks and destroying them with explosives.

In 1945 the returning U.S. forces had the unenviable task of recapturing these works from an enemy who was not disposed to surrender, and the operations (with the exception of Fort Wint, where the Japanese had moved out) were bloody in the extreme, since all the forts were liberally provided with tunnels and other underground facilities which were grimly defended. But the re-taking of Fort Drum, a little-known operation, is worth relating in some detail due to its peculiar difficulty and the unusual method employed.

The problem was simply: how to flush out a determined garrison from what amounted to a concrete castle in the middle of the bay, the only entrances to which (two 'sally ports' at the stern end) were covered by intense machine gun fire from within the fort tunnels. A naval reconnaissance vessel which approached the ports was subjected to intense fire, and it was obvious that no sort of assault would survive an attempt there. A cruiser fired 5-in. armour-piercing shells at the armoured 6-in. gun casemates on the sides of the work; the shells penetrated but did little else and did not appear to unduly upset the occupants.

Eventually a plan was determined; on the old parade

ground of Corregidor (which had been liberated by air-borne assault in February) a full-sized outline of Fort Drum was marked out, 350 feet long and 135 feet wide, and using engineer plans of the fort flown from Washington the turrets, ventilators, manholes and every other aperture on the top surface were represented by wooden dummies. Using the plans, combat engineers also determined the most effective place to locate demolition charges, paying particular attention to the location of the main magazine. Infantry and engineers were practised in dashing on to the model and taking up positions to cover every aperture with automatic rifles and machine guns while the engineers laid their charges. Finally a landing craft was procured and fitted with two 5000-gallon tanks, hoses and high-capacity centrifugal pumps, and a landing ship had a drawbridge built and attached to its conning tower — a reversion to the medieval 'beffroy' or tower necessitated by the fact that the top deck of the fort was 40 feet above the waterline.

On Friday 13th April 1945 (an auspicious day) the landing craft's tanks were filled with a mixture of two-thirds diesel oil and one-third gasoline, and the assault force sailed out to Fort Drum. Covered by naval

vessels, the landing craft was manoeuvred alongside the fort, the drawbridge was lowered, and the troops dashed on to the top of the fort to take up their rehearsed positions. Now the landing ship moved alongside, passed its hoses across, switched on its pumps, and through the hoses went the 10,000 gallons of oil and petrol, to be poured into the ventilators of the fort.

Within ten minutes the job was done. The hoses were disconnected, the fuses of the demolition charges lit, the men re-embarked, lines cut and the fleet moved away. Thirty minutes later a series of enormous explosions wrecked the fort; the 6-in. thick 12-feet square armoured roof of the main magazine was seen to sail hundreds of feet into the air and fall into the sea, and the ignition of the oil mixture generated a huge pall of smoke.

It was almost a week before the fort stopped burning and it was possible to land on it and investigate the interior; the remains of some eighty Japanese defenders were found inside. The entire work was, of course, wrecked beyond any hope of repair, and it remains today a shattered wreck.

The technique of pumping inflammable liquid in and then firing it had been pioneered some three weeks earlier in a last-resort attempt to deal with a Japanese force hidden in the mortar pits and tunnels on Fort Hughes nearby, and a similar measure was resorted to some years later by the Australian Army to deal with some extensive earthworks in a hill in Korea. Provided an assault party

Nagasaki, devastated by the second Atomic bomb. Note that the more substantial buildings in the background have resisted the blast.

can gain some aperture and take a hose with them, it is a fearsome and infallible method of putting any subterranean work out of action.

Effective as all these different methods were, they were soon overshadowed by the greatest Secret Weapon of them all, the Atomic Bomb. The effect of the two bombs dropped on Japan in August 1945 was so devastating that it was freely prophesied that no form of protection could withstand such a form of attack. And yet . . . it is interesting to speculate what a western city might have looked like after similar treatment to that meted out to Hiroshima; for the notable thing about all the pictures of Hiroshima is the way in which the few reinforced concrete buildings stand erect above the devastation which surrounds them. This was largely discounted at the time; blast, as everybody knew, does peculiar and inexplicable things.

The combination of the nuclear bomb and that other child of 1939–45, the guided missile, was the military threat (or promise) which overshadowed all else after the Second World War. What, it was asked, was the use of surrounding yourself with permanent defensive works when an enemy out of sight could send over a missile to detonate a nuclear warhead inside the defences?

Dispersal was the thing; spread everything out thinly so that there was never a sufficiently large collection of forces to justify using an expensive missile; get rid of fixed defences and the mentality that goes with them.

The first to fall to this sweeping axe was coast defence; the United States deactivated its coast defence in 1949 and Britain followed suit in 1956. Other countries also removed their coast guns and abandoned their expensive forts, though a few countries still retain them; more, one suspects, as useful accommodation and training grounds for conscript armies than for any utility as defences, for the ship-launched guided missile appears to have reached the stage where it has taken the initiative once held by the firmly-anchored coast gun.

The Maginot Line and similar works were, of course, thoroughly discredited by the events of 1939–45, and appear to have been relegated to use as stores by their various owners. But then, after the first reactions to the nuclear age began to wear off, and some carefully controlled and monitored tests of various nuclear weapons were made, second thoughts began to appear. Perhaps the nuclear weapon was not quite as all-conquering as it had been thought; perhaps fortress-type structures had a higher resistance than had been believed. Much of the results of these tests has never been publicly revealed; careful study of what has been published indicates that much of it falls into the 'instant astonishment' category designed to impress the uncritical with the might of the weapons, while large areas of investigation are not mentioned. But it would seem to the man in the street that perhaps, after all, the atomic bomb and its later cousins might not be so all-conquering.

The Swiss, for example, have not only continued the use of the underground defences begun before 1939 but have added to them in recent years. The French re-activated sections of the Maginot Line, though recent reports indicate that they are selling chunks of it to anyone who fancies a bijou villa in reinforced concrete; which indicates a reversion from Maginot's continuous line to a policy of independent redoubts. In Britain some years ago the pacifist Left made great outcry when they discovered that there were subterranean 'Regional Seats of Government' prepared against the aftermath of a possible nuclear war. In the United States the Intercontinental Ballistic Missiles which form the means of dealing with fortification are, we are told, buried in immensely thick concrete 'silos', as are many of the anti-aircraft missiles. Reports from all over the world indicate that wherever there is a fear of aerial attack with nuclear missiles, the answer has been either to disperse or, more and more, to go underground, delving deep and reinforcing the earth above with a substantial layer of concrete and steel. It may be that, in default of demonstrated proof, these defences are not as secure as their builders hope. It may be that, as a classic passage in a British Army publication of the early 1950s said, 'The best defence against the Atomic Bomb is not to be there when it goes off.' But more and more the conviction is growing that *some* defence is better than no defence. There is, by now, enough knowledge in the military

engineering world of the effects of nuclear explosions which can be married to the knowledge painstakingly (and sometimes painfully) acquired over the centuries, to be able to devise forms of construction which will protect the occupants from the weapons of an enemy, leaving him in a fit condition to utilise his own weapons when the opportunity arises. And when you come to analyse the matter, what else was fortification? The Keep, the Caponier, the Lunette, Hornwork, covered way and chemin des rondes have all passed into history. But the purpose that put them into history's pages remains; all that changes is that which has always changed – the weapons, the tactics, the systems of attack and defence;

and as we have seen, this has been a continuing process throughout the ages. We are, in the fortification sense, going through the same sort of revolution which occurred in the fifteenth century after the invention of gunpowder, and there is every reason to believe that, in due course, the way will become more clear and a method of defence will evolve. There is only one unchanging fact of fortification; that the factor that counts in the last analysis is not the quality of the work itself, but the quality of the garrison inside.

A Titan I.C.B.M. being launched from a 146-foot deep underground silo. *Keystone*.

Glossary

Abattis. An obstacle formed of felled trees, with their trimmed and sharpened branches facing the enemy. They may be placed in the ditch, where the escarp is a gentle slope, or on the country side of the glacis.

Advanced Glacis. A Secondary glacis outside the primary, usually in conjunction with abattis and trous-de-loup.

Arrow. A small outwork of trench and parapet placed in the salient angle of the glacis and connected to the covered way by a short passage.

Arrowhead Bastion. A Bastion with the orillons severely cut back or recessed into the flanks, so as to make the gorge narrow and thus exhibit an arrowhead form in plan view.

Bailey. An enclosed space in a castle site, generally in front of the mound, in which the domestic offices of the castle were sited and in which retainers lived and worked. It served as the primary line of defence.

Banquette. A platform behind the parapet on which the soldier stands to fire, so that he may step down after firing and thus be completely protected by the parapet. Later became more frequently known as the fire-step.

Barbette. Sometimes applied to a raised gun platform behind the parapet, similar to the terreplein but of limited size for a small number of guns. A gun or battery is said to be EN BARBETTE when it is placed so as to fire over a low parapet without embrasure; the term is said to have derived from the French, due to the resemblance of the parapet to a beard beneath the gun muzzle.

Bastion. A work composed of two faces and two flanks and forming part of the major work. Bastions are joined by curtains and are constructed in order that the whole escarp may be seen.

Bastioned Head. A face of a work which is deeply indented.

Batardeau. A masonry dam, 7–8 feet thick, crossing the whole breadth of the ditch opposite the flanked angles and bastions. It retains water in those sections of the ditch required to be flooded.

Battlement. Popular term for machicolation, the construction of a wall parapet with alternate high and low sections: the defenders could thus discharge weapons over the low sections and seek cover behind the high sections.

Beffroy. A tower structure built in order to assist attacking troops to reach the top of a wall. May have been constructed at the point of assault or on wheels or rollers and pushed to the required point.

Berm. A space or path sometimes left between the top of the escarp and the foot of the rampart. It serves as a communication around the work and also stops earth from the rampart falling into the ditch.

Bombing Trench. An auxiliary trench dug behind the fire (or 'front line') trench at a suitable distance to permit grenades to be thrown from it into the fire trench. Manned by skilled grenade-throwers its purpose was to allow raiding parties entering the fire trench to be bombarded with grenades.

Bonnette.
a) A small earthwork raised above the parapet in order to shield the banquette from enfilade fire.
b) A work placed before the salient angle of a ravelin.

Breastwork. See **Parapet**.

Caponier. A work defending a ditch by extending into it or across it, and enabling fire to be brought to bear on the width of the ditch.

Carnot Wall. A detached wall in front of the rampart, separated from it by a chemin des rondes, the wall being built with arched niches on the rear face to protect the men defending it.

Casemate. A vaulted chamber in the rampart with a port to permit artillery to be fired from it.

Cavalier. A defensible work on the terreplein of a bastion and of similar trace to the bastion; or a defensible work on the terreplein of the curtain. Its use is to command some rising ground within cannon range and to act as a traverse to prevent the adjacent curtain from being enfiladed.

Chemin Couvert. See **Covered Way**.

Chemin des Rondes. A species of covered way between a fausse braye and the rampart for the assembly and movement of troops.

Cheval de Frise. An obstacle in the form of a joist of timber about 12 feet long, with pointed iron-shod stakes protruding from the sides. Placed on the ground, the lower stakes act as legs, while those at the top and sides form the obstacle, notably against cavalry. First recorded in 1658 at the Siege of Groningen in Friesland, from whence came the name 'The Friesland Horse'.

Citadel. A fort forming part of the works of a town and fortified both towards the town and towards the country. It should always be on the most commanding ground, and should the town be taken it becomes a retreat for the garrison.

Command. The vertical elevation of one work above another or above the surrounding country; the height of the crest of the parapet.

Communication Trench. A trench dug for the purpose of moving troops, ammunition, rations etc, from the rear areas to the fire trench without exposing them to enemy observation or fire.

Cordon. A semi-circular projection of stone whose diameter is about one foot, placed nearly at the top of the revetment of the escarp. It throws off the drip of rain and also acts as an obstacle to escalade.

Counterfort. Buttresses or earth ramparts added to the inner side of an older wall in order to make it more resistant.

Counterguard. An earthwork having two faces which form a salient angle; the angle is not so acute as that of a ravelin and the gorge is not closed. Generally placed opposite the bastion or ravelin to prevent the opposite flanks from being seen from the covered way.

Counterscarp. The exterior wall of the ditch below the glacis.

Counterscarp Gallery. A passage behind the counterscarp wall, with loopholes, allowing fire to be brought to bear on the ditch in the rear of the attackers.

Couvre-Face. An earthwork equivalent to a Carnot Wall.

Crémaillère. A front or face with receding 'steps' to permit greater flanking fire.

Crownwork. A work composed of a bastion between two curtains, which are terminated by half-bastions. It is joined to the major work by two long sides.

Covered Way. A space between the top of the counterscarp and the glacis which allows troops to form for defence or for a sortie.

Cunette. A small ditch cut in the middle of a dry ditch in order to drain off rainwater.

Curtain. That part of the rampart lying between two bastions and joining their flanks.

Demilune. See **Ravelin.**

Ditch. An excavation in front of the rampart; it may be WET or DRY.

Embrasure. An opening in the parapet to allow artillery to fire. It is subdivided as follows:
Throat: the interior opening, no wider than is necessary to admit the gun muzzle.
Mouth: the exterior opening, governed by the amount of lateral coverage required.
Sole: the bottom surface, the outward slope of which is governed by the minimum range of the gun. In cases where the gun is reserved for indirect or high-angle fire, the slope is inwards.
Cheek: the side walls of the embrasure.

Epaulement. A parapet thrown up in advance of a ditch; usually a field expedient.

Escarp. The inner wall or face of the ditch, below the rampart.

Esplanade. A place of even ground, clear of buildings, between a citadel and a town, so that no approach can be made without being seen from the citadel.

Exterior Slope. The forward face of a parapet or rampart.

Faces. The faces of a work are those parts which form a salient angle projecting towards the country.

Fausse Braye. An advanced parapet before the main rampart, leaving a space, or Chemin des Rondes, between it and the rampart.

Fieldwork. A defensive work prepared 'in the field', i.e. a work built hastily in the course of a campaign or battle to serve a limited function. Usually applied to trenches and minor obstacles.

Fire-Step. See **Banquette.**

Fire Trench. The most forward line of entrenchment in a defensive system, that which is the first continuous line of defence. More popularly known as the Front Line Trench.

Flank. That part of a work so disposed as to protect another.

Flèche. See **Arrow.**

Fraises. Palisades placed in a horizontal position at the top of the escarp and counterscarp to form an obstacle against escalade.

Front. A Front of Fortification consists of two bastions and the curtain between.

Gabion. An open-ended cylinder, generally of woven brushwood but sometimes of interlaced iron bands, wire netting etc, which could be filled with earth and used to revet or reinforce the sides of excavations, especially in fieldworks, to prevent trenches or ditches caving-in during wet weather.

Genouillère. The section of parapet beneath an embrasure. Generally referred to by its height (e.g. a 3 ft. 6 in. Genouillère), it is a necessary factor in the design or selection of gun carriages for a particular work.

Glacis. An elevated mound of earth on the country side of the ditch, sloping outward in a continuation of the Superior Slope, so that an enemy attacking the ditch must move up it and thus be exposed to fire from the parapet.

Gorge. The rear face of a work.

Haxo Casemate. A casemate formed in the parapet, arched with masonry and covered with earth, and open in the rear to the terreplein.

Hornwork.
a) A work to defend a point, such as a bridge, consisting of a bastioned front with flanks extending back to an obstacle, e.g. a river.
b) A work comprised of two half-bastions and a curtain, with two long sides, paralleling the faces of ravelins or bastions so as to be defended by them.

Interior Slope. The inclination of the earth of a rampart nearest to the town, i.e. on the inside of the rampart. (Or) The line of fall between the crest of the parapet and the banquette or between the banquette and the plane of construction.

Keep. The stronghold and residential part of a castle; by extension, an independent self-defensible structure within a fort.

Lines of Crémaillère. An obliquely cut face.

Lunette.
a) A redan to which flanks or lateral wings have been added.
b) Works to flank a ravelin, one face being perpendicular to the face of the ravelin and the other to the face of a bastion.

Merlons. Those portions of a parapet between the embrasures.

Moat. Common usage for Ditch: the excavation around a fort or work.

Motte. A mound, natural or artificial, surmounted by a palisade and keep, and forming the nucleus of a Norman castle.

Orillon. The part of the bastion near the shoulder which prevents the retired flank from being seen obliquely.

Palisade. An obstacle of wooden posts planted in the ditch.

Parados. An embankment or other construction of earth or masonry behind a defensive position to prevent reverse fire from being brought to bear.

Parallel. A trench excavated by a besieging force parallel with the face or faces of the work under siege. Successive parallels were excavated, each being nearer to the work and connected by saps (q.v.) until the final parallel was sufficiently close to allow it to be used as a starting point for the assault on the place.

Parapet. A bank of earth over which a soldier may fire. In permanent works it crowns the rampart. Also known as a breastwork.

Place of Arms. Space formed in the covered way. SALIENT Places of Arms are the open spaces between the circular parts of the counterscarp and the prolongation of the intersection of the branches of the covered way. They are for the assembly of troops destined for the defence of the covered way. RE-ENTERING Places of Arms are constructed within the two faces so as to flank the branches and contain defensive troops.

Plane of Construction. The natural level of the site, from which command is calculated.

Queue d'Hironde. A work composed of two redans, the re-entering faces defending each other. Also known as a DOUBLE REDAN.

Ramp. A roadway cut into the interior slope of the rampart and forming a communication between the plain of construction and the terreplein.

Rampart. A bank of earth behind the ditch, on top of which is formed the parapet. This gives greater command to the parapet. The rampart is generally built from the earth excavated in the construction of the ditch.

Ravelin. A work constructed outside the curtain, of two faces meeting in a salient angle, with two demi-gorges formed by the counterscarp. It is used to cover the curtain, the gates, and the flanks of a bastion. Also known as a DEMI-LUNE.

Redan. A work of two faces forming a salient angle.

Redoubt. A closed, independent work, of square or polygonal trace, without bastions.

Re-Entering. Term denoting the movement of the trace inwards; the opposite of Salient.

Relief. The height of any point of the work above a datum, which may be the plane of construction (in which case it is termed CONSTRUCTIVE RELIEF) or the bottom of the ditch (in which case it is termed ABSOLUTE RELIEF).

Revetment. The masonry faces retaining the earth sides of the ditch or parapet. Generally constructed with the front face sloping at one-twentieth of the height, and the rear face constructed in steps increasing 6 inches in thickness every 18 inches from the top.

Rifle Pit. Small trench, especially for one man, sufficiently deep to allow the soldier to stand in and fire a rifle across the top edge. Now generally superseded by the term 'slit trench'.

Sally Ports. Openings cut in the glacis at the faces of the re-entering places of arms and at the branches of the covered way, to allow raiding parties to leave the work and regain it.

Sap. A trench extended forward from a parallel with the intention of either constructing a fresh parallel or forming a starting point for an assault.

Sap and Parallel. System of besieging a place, attributed to Vauban, by the alternate excavations of parallels and saps so that the assaulting troops could be brought close to the place but remain under cover the while.

Sap-Head. The end of a sap, at which point it is either extended sideways to form a fresh parallel, or brought to the surface of the ground to afford an exit for an assaulting party.

Shell Keep. A keep built not as a solid unit but rather as a curtain wall with buildings on the inner side, the centre of the keep being an open space.

Shoulder of Bastion. The junction of the face and flank of a bastion: an expression used only in the setting-out or planning of a work, since it forms a locus or reference point for the alignment or siting of other parts of the work.

Superior Slope. The crest of the parapet, facing outwards.

Tenaille.
a) A work consisting of two faces and a small curtain constructed between the flanks of the bastion, in front of the curtain.
b) The reverse of a redan — two faces forming a re-entering angle.

Tenailled Head. An indented face to a work.

Tenaillon. A work at the side of a ravelin similar to a lunette but differing in the alignment of its faces.

Terreplein. An enlarged banquette behind the rampart, formed for the reception of artillery to fire over the parapet.

Tower Bastion. A bastion in the form of a defensible tower, having rooms and casemates within which cover the ditch. Attributed to Vauban.

Traverse. An earthwork of equal height to the crest of the parapet and running into the work in order to prevent the banquette from being swept by enfilade fire.

Trous-de-Loup. Holes, 6–8 feet deep and of similar diameter, with sharpened stakes at the bottom, dug to form obstacles. Usually positioned in advance of the glacis, the earth excavated in their construction helping to form the glacis.

Work. A general term for a work of defence, i.e. a fort or lesser structure.

Index

Entries in **Bold Type** refer to illustrations.